Down The Last Road

Down The Last Road

The Last Day Of The Earthly Life Of Jesus

Richard P. Zimmerman

NOVO CIVITAS BOOKS AND RESOURCES • SEATTLE, WASHINGTON

DOWN THE LAST ROAD

The Last Day Of The Earthly Life Of Jesus

Novo Civitas_LLC_ Books and Resources
Novocivitas.com

Copyright © 2021 by Richard P. Zimmerman

All rights reserved. No part of this book may be reproduced in any form without the written permission of the author, with the exception of brief excerpts for the purpose of review.

God made One who knew no sin to be sin on our behalf, so that we might become God's righteousness in him.

2 Corinthians 5:21

Contents

1	Day Of Sorrows	1
2	Four Writers, One Story	9
3	The Last Day Of The Earthly Life Of Jesus	19
4	Study Notes	61
5	Using This Resource	119
6	About This Translation	131
	In Gratitude	143
	References	147

1

Day Of Sorrows

Day Of Sorrows

One day of sorrow stands out from all others. We sing about that day nearly every Sunday when we gather for worship. We only need one word to signify that entire day of agony. It is the symbol of Christianity, and it is one word that sums up the day that stands out from all others: *cross*. The cross represents the most physical element of the suffering of Jesus. But it also stands for the greater pain of the entire day. Blow by blow, through betrayal, abandonment and humiliation, Jesus endured to the end of that day of sorrow.

It is a day that stands out from all others, but it is not a day that stands *above* all others. Easter is a day above the day of the cross. Easter is that decisive hinge on which everything else depends. Easter is that instant when life burst forth out of the cavern of death. But Easter was made possible by the grueling 24 hours of Jesus's dying day. The day of the cross is the day when Jesus willingly received the worst pain and suffering the world could offer and absorbed it all into the infinite pool of his endless grace.

In a communion meditation, Lloyd Ogilvie once said, "It is astonishing, isn't it, that all the enemies in life and death have been defeated through Jesus Christ's life and death. Fear of any eventuality, even our own death, can not destroy us. He has done all things to set us free to live the abundant life."[1]

It is, in fact, so astonishing as to be nearly beyond the grasp of our ordinary experience. Even though my mind might have accepted the truth of it, even though my heart may have felt the power of it, even if I have committed my will to following the way of Jesus, I still might have difficulty experiencing that freedom on a daily basis. Many people of sincere faith feel the liberation offered by Jesus only now and then. Or maybe they never feel it completely in a way that lasts through every circumstance. While some part of our spirits has received the gift of eternal life, most of us still live in fear of death and under the weight of doubt. We are separated from our liberated selves by the daily struggle to hang on to what we know is true. In short we don't *feel* liberated, and we don't *feel* the abundant life.

Some consolation for our lagging feelings comes in the Gospel reports. All of the disciples and friends of Jesus responded to the event of the arrest of Jesus by running away, skulking in darkness, weeping, and hiding. Apparently the astonishing truth of what Jesus was doing did not make them feel great courage or transcendent peace in those terrifying moments when everything seemed to be falling apart. Even though they had been with Jesus for years, even though they heard his teaching and watched him heal the sick, even though they ate the bread he offered and drank the cup he gave to them, the disciples still lost their courage when Jesus was

---

[1] Lloyd John Ogilvie, *The Cup of Wonder: Communion Meditations*, 140.

arrested and taken off for his trial. All this happened within hours after the last supper–the event which most Christians regard as a supreme encouragement. How could it be that the calories their bodies used to flee in terror were supplied by the bread and wine of communion? As it was for those first followers, so it has been for many if not all of us who followed later: people who have faith in Jesus struggle with lagging feelings.

And this lag points to one of the central purposes of the Christian life: spiritual growth. On a daily basis we don't automatically feel calm and brave even after we have received his grace. But intentional spiritual growth is a process of taking actions to help our thoughts and feelings catch up with our faith. Discipleship means taking steps to inform your mind and heart of what your faith says is true.

Faith is different from feelings. And we should not be surprised when our feelings lag behind our faith. Do you long for the truth of your faith to have a greater impact on your daily experience? This book is designed to bring the experience of the Gospel narratives of the last day of the life of Jesus into focused awareness so that daily life is transformed into a steady experience of liberation.

Of course, the last day of the earthly life of Jesus is filled with hopelessness, death, and despair. So why would an intense focus on those last 24 hours strengthen anyone's faith?

The death of Jesus only matters to our faith because of the resurrection. As Luke Timothy Johnson has written,

> If Jesus is simply dead, there are any number of ways in which we can relate ourselves to his life and his accomplishments. And we might even, if some obscure bit of data should turn up, hope to learn more about him. But we cannot reasonably expect to learn more *from* him.
>
> If he is alive, however, everything changes. It is no longer a matter of our questioning a historical record, but a matter of our being put in question by one who has broken every rule of ordinary human existence. If Jesus lives, then it must be as life-giver. Jesus is not simply a figure of the past in that case, but a person in the present; not merely a memory that we can analyze and manipulate, but an agent who can confront and instruct us. What we learn *about* him must therefore include what we continue to learn *from* him.
>
> To be a Christian means to assert that Jesus is alive, is indeed life-giving Spirit (I Cor. 15:45).[2]

Daily events tend to obscure that reality. We get caught up in whatever is happening in our lives or in the world around us and we lose sight of the reality of this core truth of our faith. That is why it is essential to build in daily, weekly, and annual practices that put us back into communion with Jesus.

And yet to follow along the path of these 24 hours in the life of Jesus is heartbreaking and jarring. To truly reflect on how lonely the path was that Jesus walked on Good Friday is almost unbearable. The evening before, at the meal we call "the last supper," he offered himself to his friends at the table in the upper room. This was a tremendously intimate act. Hours later

---

[2] Luke Timothy Johnson, *Living Jesus: Learning the Heart of the Gospel*, 4-5.

in the garden, when the soldiers had him surrounded, Jesus secured the release of his disciples by asking the soldiers to let them go. He thus saved his friends from joining him in death. The guards consented to his request and did not arrest them. This is what that last day in the life of Jesus was all about. His capture secured our release. His trial and punishment removed the accusations from our record. No one else could do this for us. He had to walk the road of suffering alone.

But in every moment we have the chance to reverse that loneliness by walking with him. This is most pointedly true on Good Friday when we walk the road to the cross in our minds and remember what he suffered so that we might live in freedom and abundance forever.

A Day In Bible Time

"And there was evening, and there was morning, the first day."
   -Genesis 1:5 b.

We generally think of the beginning of a day as midnight. Sometimes we consider dawn the start of a day. Genesis says that God created light out of darkness. Darkness precedes light, so a day begins in the evening at sunset and proceeds through the next 24 hours, concluding at the following twilight. So the last day of the life of Jesus, from the point of view of the Bible's system of counting days, begins right before the last supper and ends as the friends of Jesus lay his body in the tomb.

Down The Last Road

When Jesus woke up on Thursday morning, the day before his crucifixion, it is probable that he knew he would never sleep again in his earthly body. He knew that he would share his last Passover meal that evening with his disciples. He knew that Judas would betray him, and he knew that once the plot of his execution was in motion it would be hurried along so that he would be dead before sundown on Friday evening.

So as Jesus sent his disciples into Jerusalem to arrange for a Passover meal, he was poised on the edge of his last day of life in his earthly body. The sunset before the meal marked the beginning of his last day. He knew his hour had come. He knew that God would bring light out of darkness by what would happen in the coming day.

So much changed on that day. Surprising twists and turns punctuate a tumultuous sequence of events. It may seem as though it would be impossible to reconstruct one unified account, given all that took place on that day. How could all four reports from that day be reconciled with one another? Now that so many years have gone by since that day, how can we really know what took place?

The answers to those questions came in careful study of how four writers gave us one story.

2

Four Writers, One Story

Four Writers, One Story

Four voices narrate the last 24 hours of the life of Jesus. The four Gospels tell what happened in far greater detail than at any other time in his life. There is tremendous unity in their reports, as their narratives link the hours of that day together.

But it is not easy to see the one story of that one day by simply picking up your Bible and reading. These are four independent accounts. They cover the same events but they rarely describe things in the exact same way.

I have created an original translation of these sections of the four Gospels, while at the same time blending their four voices into one continuous story. I was careful not to add anything of my own, and I made every effort to include every detail narrated by these four about those last hours. As far as possible, without altering the text in any way, I have taken their words and arranged them in an order that makes a whole and complete narrative.

The Struggle To Read The Bible

I am deeply aware of how great a struggle it can be to simply read the Bible. While I eventually became an avid reader of the Bible as I was growing up, I still remember the feeling of wanting to read the Bible, knowing I should read the Bible, but never really being able to simply open to a section of my Bible and read for any length of time.

Over the years I have encountered many sincere, intelligent, and well-educated people who quietly have confessed to me that they have a hard time reading their Bibles. Even people who love certain passages and who have memorized inspiring verses have a hard time just sitting down and reading it for an extended period of time.

So as a pastor I have always looked for ways to draw people into the experience of the Bible. If people are immersed in the story, they will eventually love the experience. The events of the life of Jesus will sweep them up into God's grand narrative. This is especially true for these last events of his life. Knowing that Jesus endured so much pain and suffering out of love for me is essential to understanding his invitation to forgiveness and new life. Yet something even greater than simply knowing the details is needed. We have to find a way to consider the whole narrative.

Surely this is the most important story ever told. Living entirely within the love of his heavenly Father, Jesus turned his face toward the cross and allowed himself to be subjected to unfathomable agonies, physical and spiritual. So I gave myself this challenge: could I faithfully convey that story so that people will hear, understand, and respond to this great offer of love?

Several years ago I began to think about how I could present the narrative of this last day in order to create the experience of being with Jesus for the people of my community. Over the years I tried various approaches to Maundy Thursday and Good Friday with varying degrees of success.

One year, around the time of Easter, I became aware of the television series *"24."* The series *"24"* was a somewhat revolutionary television drama. A whole television season of 24 episodes was entirely created out of the events of one single day. Each hour of the day was presented as events in real time. Viewers were taken on a wild ride through one intense day in the life of the main character in weekly one-hour installments. It makes for pretty entertaining television if you don't think too hard about the practical improbabilities.

I began to think about what might happen if this same approach was applied to Jesus's last day. The intensity of the last 24 hours in the life of Jesus is both more real and more emotionally dramatic than most people realize. He was not allowed to sleep. Each and every one of those 24 hours was jammed full of events. I began to wonder if I could place all of those details into 24 one-hour vignettes. So I studied the four Gospels to see how their reports fit together on a 24 hour timeline. What an experience to immerse myself into the episodes that make up those last 24 hours. Each moment was intense and full of detail. I did not want to impose my own suppositions on the narratives. Clearly, a new hit television drama was not likely to result from this thought experiment. And yet I began to wonder what might emerge if the story of those last 24 hours of the life of Jesus were told without filling in anything through my own suppositions and guesses. Might the Gospels themselves provide all of the necessary detail?

Down The Last Road

The more I read the Gospels side by side, the more it did seem possible to develop a unified narrative of everything that took place on that day, without redundancy, and without inserting anything of my own.

I created this composite translation of the biblical accounts of those 24 hours so that readers would be able to simply progress through everything the Bible says about these events without the distractions. The actual words of Matthew, Mark, Luke and John have been spliced together into one unified narrative.

To my knowledge, no one has ever completed a blended translation quite like this.[3] From as early as 172 AD various attempts have been made to harmonize the Gospels.[4] This has been considered controversial at times.[5]

My blended translation is, to the best of my ability, a juxtaposition of the four Gospels as they report those last 24 hours of the life of Jesus. This may have been inappropriate in the ancient world when Bibles were scarce, hand-copied, and prone to forgery and error. But we live in a time when the accuracy of a document can be easily checked in multiple ways.

---

[3] In their book, *Jesus Christ: The Greatest Life*, Cheney Johnston and Stanley Ellisen have undertaken an effort similar to what I have done in my blended translation. Their approach is to be commended in its comprehensive nature. They have completed this juxtaposition for the whole of all four Gospels. Their book is an excellent source for study.

[4] David A. deSilva, *Introduction To The New Testament*, 148.

[5] Oscar Cullmann, *Plurality*, 49.

So this meditational version is offered as an assistance to readers for the sake of spending uninterrupted time with Jesus in his last hours.

The result is a wonderfully detailed account of what happened on that day. I always followed the axiom, *When in doubt, believe each writer.* So this blended account contains everything those four wrote in a smooth narrative.

This is in no way meant to replace the reading of the standard translations of the Bible. I simply put the accounts together in this form as a way of helping you live through those 24 hours with Jesus in your mind and in your heart. If any element of my narrative strikes you as odd, or out of place, or inaccurate to what you believe happened, then I urge you to get out your own Bible and read the sections in question.

My belief in the essential unity of the four Gospels is not a new idea. John Calvin's commentary on the gospels is presented as a harmony of the first three Gospels followed by a commentary on the Gospel of John. In that commentary he wrote,

> John is believed to have written chiefly with the intention of maintaining the Divinity of Christ . . . But whatever might be his motive for writing at that time, there can be no doubt whatever that God intended a far higher benefit for his Church. He therefore dictated to the Four Evangelists what they should write, in such a manner that, while each had his own part assigned to him, the whole might be collected into one body; and it is our duty now to blend the Four by a mutual relation, so that we may

permit ourselves to be taught by all of them, as by one mouth.[6]

This seems all the more urgently true as we consider the last hours of Jesus in his earthly life.

The Value Of This Story

About twelve years passed from when I first considered compiling some form of narrative of the Good Friday events until I finally completed this blended translation. As I pressed on to the end I was continuously motivated by the hope that people would read these words in their entirety at one time, and that the impact of the whole narrative would become an experience of discipleship. It was my hope that people would come to understand more clearly what God is doing in the world and would be better equipped to share Jesus's message of love, forgiveness, hope, and transformation with those around them.

There is tremendous value to be able to place each event on the clock. Picture yourself walking into an upper room in Jerusalem with mixed feelings of anticipation for celebration of the Passover but also with worries about the growing tensions between the authorities and our little movement. And then imagine sitting alone at sunset that next day and despairing. So many things had gone wrong so fast. Any happy thought about the Passover just 24 hours earlier was entirely wiped away. As you will see when you read, all of the details in the four

---

[6] Calvin, *Commentary On The Gospel of John*, 22.

accounts fit together beautifully like a joint fashioned by a skilled carpenter. A careful study of these texts has made me trust that we have remarkably accurate accounts of these 24 hours in the life of Jesus.

The blended translation is presented in a simple, uncluttered format. Following the complete narrative of those 24 hours I have included extensive notes regarding the Gospels and my method of blending their reports. Trust that all of your questions can be posed later by examining the *Study Notes* and the description of my process of translation and blending that follows. While the simple story is the main reason I created this book, I didn't feel that I could just print that simple text all by itself because so many questions arise about the origin of such a narrative. *What parts of the Bible were used? How did this come to be?* The *Study Notes* are meant to answer all of those questions. It is hoped that the simple form of the text in chapter two and the *Study Notes* in chapter three may serve as two sides of understanding.

Please release yourself to the reading of the narrative. This resource was created so that the truth of what Jesus did can become a greater and more enduring part of your daily experience. It presents an immersive experience into the very words of the Gospel writers as they tell the details of the suffering of Jesus. Concentrate on being with Jesus in the story. He is there with you.

3

The Last Day Of The Earthly Life Of Jesus

The Last Day Of The Earthly Life Of Jesus

In the first month, on the fourteenth day of the month, at twilight, is the Passover to the Lord.

Leviticus 23:5

Preparations For The Evening Meal

When the day of unleavened bread came, the day on which the Passover lamb had to be sacrificed, Jesus sent two of his disciples, Peter and John, and he told them, "Go prepare a place for us to eat the Passover."

Matthew 26:17-19
Mark 14:12-16
Luke 22:7-13

They asked, "Where should we prepare it?"

He answered, "When you enter the city gate you will see a man carrying a pitcher of water; follow him and where he enters a house you will follow him in. Tell the owner of the house, "The Teacher says, 'My time is near. I am going to observe the Passover with my disciples at your house. Where is the guest room where I am to eat the Passover with my disciples?'

"He will show you a spacious room on an upper floor, furnished. Prepare for us there."

They went and found everything as he said, so they got everything ready for the Passover.

Twilight – At The Table

Matthew 26:20
John 13:1-17

When evening came Jesus was reclining at the table with the Twelve. It was just before the Passover Feast. Jesus knew that the time had come for him to leave this world and go to the Father. Having loved his own who were in the world, he now showed them the full measure of his love.

The meal was being served, and the devil had already put into the heart Judas Iscariot, son of Simon, to betray Jesus. Knowing that the Father had given everything into his hands, and that he had been sent by God and was returning to God, Jesus got up from the meal, took off his outer clothes, took a towel, and wrapped it around his waist. Then he poured water into a basin. He began to wash his disciples' feet, and he dried them with the towel he had wrapped around himself.

Then he came toward Simon Peter, who said to him, "Lord, are you going to wash my feet?"

Jesus replied, "You do not understand now what I am doing, but you will understand later."

"Certainly not," declared Peter, "you will never wash my feet."

Jesus answered, "If I don't wash your feet you have no part in me."

"Then, Lord," Simon Peter replied, "not only my feet but also my hands and my head!"

Jesus answered, "A person who has had a bath needs only to wash the feet; the rest of the body is clean. And you are clean, though not all of you," because he knew who would betray him, and that was why he said *you are not all clean.*

And so when he had finished washing feet he put his outer clothes back on and reclined again in his place. "Can you comprehend what I have just done for you? You call me 'Teacher' and 'Lord,' which is right, because that is who I am. Since I, your Lord and Teacher, have washed your feet, you should also wash each other's feet. I have set an example for you to do for one another what I have done for you. I am telling you the truth; no servant is greater than his master. No messenger is greater than the one who sent the message. Now that you have learned this, you will be blessed if you do it."

Bread And Cup

Then Jesus said to them, "I have deeply desired to eat this Passover with you before I suffer. For I tell you, I will not eat it again until it finds fulfillment in the kingdom of God."

Luke 22:15-20
Matthew 26:26-29
Mark 14:22-25
I Corinthians 11:23-25

While they were eating, Jesus took bread, gave thanks and broke it, gave it to his disciples, and said, "Take and eat; this is my body broken for you. Do this in remembrance of me."

Then he took the cup, gave thanks and offered it to them, saying, "Drink from it, all of you. This is my blood of the new covenant, which is poured out for many for the forgiveness of sins. Do this, whenever you drink it, as a way of remembering me.

Jesus Predicts The Betrayal

Matthew 26:21-24
Mark 14:18-21
Luke 22:21-23
John 13:21-30

Jesus was deeply troubled in spirit and he solemnly declared, "I tell you truly, one of you is going to betray me."

His disciples looked around at one another, completely uncertain as to which of them he meant. They were very sad and began to say to him one after another, "Surely not I, Lord?"

One disciple, one whom Jesus loved, was reclining next to him. Simon Peter motioned to that disciple and said, "Ask him who he means."

So the disciple leaned back toward Jesus and asked, "Lord, who?"

Jesus answered, "The one who has dipped his hand into the bowl with me will betray me. The Son of Man will die just as it is written. But such misery will fall upon that man who betrays the Son of Man! It would be better if he had never been born. I will dip bread in a bowl and give it to the one who will betray me."

Then he dipped the bread and gave it to Judas Iscariot, son of Simon. As soon as Judas took the bread, Satan entered into him.

"Hurry and do what you are about to do," Jesus told him, but no one else at the table understood why Jesus said this.

The Last Day Of The Earthly Life Of Jesus

Since Judas was in charge of the money, some thought Jesus was telling him to buy things necessary for the festival or to give a gift to the poor. As soon as Judas received the bread he went out into the night.

A Dispute About Who Is Greatest

An argument began among them about which of them ought to be regarded as the greatest. Jesus said to them, "Kings lord it over their nations and those who exert authority over others call themselves 'doers of good.' But that is not how it is with you. Instead, the greatest among you will be like the youngest, and the one who leads as the one who serves. For who is ordinarily considered greater, the one who sits at the table or the one who serves? Is it not the one who sits at the table? But I am with you as one who serves. Through all my trials you are the ones who have stood by me. Just as my Father gave me rightful reign I also confer on you a kingdom. You will eat and drink at my table in my kingdom and sit on thrones, ruling the twelve tribes of Israel."

Luke 22:24-30

Jesus Predicts Simon Peter Will Deny Him

With Judas gone, Jesus said, "The Son of Man is now glorified and God is glorified in him. If God is glorified in him, God will glorify the Son in himself, and

Matthew 26:31-35
Mark 14:30-31
Luke 22:31-34
John 13:31-38

will glorify him at once.

"Children, I am with you for only a little while longer. You will look for me, and I tell you now, just as I told the Judeans, you cannot follow me to where I am now going.

"So I give you a new command: Love one another. As I have loved you, you must love one another. Everyone will know that you are my disciples because you love one another."

Simon Peter asked, "Lord, where are you going?"

Jesus answered him, "You cannot follow where I am going now but you will follow me later."

"Simon, Simon, pay attention! Satan has requested to sift you as wheat. But I have prayed that your faith may not fail you, Simon. And when you return, strengthen your brothers."

Peter answered, "Lord, why can't I follow you now? I am prepared to go to prison with you and even to die. Even if everyone scatters because of you, I never will."

But Jesus said, "Peter, will you really lay down your life for me? I must tell you, before the rooster crows twice today, you will deny you know me three times."

But Peter repeated insistently, "Even if I die with you, I will never deny you." All the other disciples also said the same thing.

What Is Needed For This New Mission

Luke 22:35-38

Then Jesus asked, "When I sent you out without a wallet, a bag or sandals, did you lack anything?"

"Nothing," they answered.

He said to them, "But now if you have money, take it, and also a bag. And if you don't have a sword, sell your cloak and buy one. As it is written in the scriptures: 'And he was counted among the rebels;' I tell you this will come true in me. Yes, what is written about me is coming to fulfillment."

The disciples said, "Here, Lord, look. We have two swords."

"That is enough," he replied.

Jesus Teaches The Disciples At The Table

"Do not let your hearts be anxious. Trust in God and trust in me. There are many rooms in my Father's house. If it were not so, I would never have told you that I am going to prepare a place for you. Since I am going to prepare a place for you, I will come back and take you to be with me so that we can be together. You know where I am going and you know the way." John 14:1-31

Thomas said, "We don't know were you are going, Lord, so how could we know the way?"

Jesus answered, "I am the way, and the truth, and the life. No one comes to the Father except through me. If you knew me, you would also know my Father. From now on, you know him and have seen him."

Philip said to him, "Lord, show us the Father and that will satisfy us."

Jesus said to him, "Even after I have been with you such a long time, Philip, don't you know me? The one who has seen me has seen the Father. How is it that you say, 'Show us the

Father?' Don't you believe that I am in the Father, and the Father is in me? The words I say to you are not just my own. But the Father, living in me, is doing his work. Believe me when I say that I am in the Father and the Father is in me, or else put your faith in me based on the evidence of the miracles themselves. I tell you the truth, anyone who has faith in me will do what I have been doing, and will do even greater things than these, because I go to the Father. And whatever you ask in my name I will do, so that the Son will bring glory to the Father. If you ask for anything in my name I will do it.

"If you love me, you will obey what I command. And I will ask the Father, and he will give you another Counselor to be with you in all times and ages—the Spirit of truth. This world is unable to receive him because it neither sees him nor knows him. You know him because he stays with you and will be in you. I will not leave you abandoned. I will come to you. Soon the world will no longer see me but you will see me. Because I live you will also live. On that day you will know that I am in my Father, and you are in me, and I am in you. Whoever has my commands and obeys them–that is the one who loves me. And those who love me will be loved by my Father, and I too will love them and show myself to them."

Then Judas (now this was not Judas Iscariot) said, "Why do you intend to reveal yourself to us, Lord, and not to the world?"

Jesus answered and said to him, "Those who love me will obey my words and my Father will love them. We will come to them and make our home with them. Anyone who does not love me will not regard my words. And these words you hear are not my own but my Father's who sent me.

"This all I have told you while still with you. But the Father will send the Counselor in my name, the Holy Spirit, who will teach you everything and will cause you to remember all the things I have said to you. I leave peace with you. I give my peace to you. But I do not give as the world gives. So do not let your hearts be anxious and do not be fearful.

"You heard me say, 'I am going away and I will come back to you.' If you loved me you would be glad that I told you I am going to the Father, for my Father is greater than I. I have told you before these things take place so that you will believe when it all does happen. I will not say much more because the ruler of this world is coming. He holds no power over me but this all is happening in order for the world to learn that I love the Father and that I do just as my Father has commanded me."

Departing From The Upper Room

Jesus then said, "Get up. We're going away from this place now." Luke 22:39
John 14:31b.

When they had sung a hymn, Jesus went out as usual to the Mount of Olives and his disciples came with him.

Down The Last Road

Teaching Along The Way From The Upper Room To The Wadi Kidron

Matthew 26:31-32
John 15:1-17:26

"I am the true vine and my Father is the vine-keeper. All of the branches in me that bear no fruit he cuts off, and he prunes every branch that does bear fruit so that it will bear even more fruit. You have been pruned by the things I have told you. Abide in me, and I will remain in you. Just as no branch can produce fruit by itself but it must remain in the vine, in that same way you cannot produce fruit unless you remain in me.

"I am the vine, you are the branches. Those who remain in me and I in them will produce large crops of fruit. You can do nothing apart from me. The one who does not remain in me is like a cast off branch that withers. Workers pick up those branches, throw them into the fire, and they are burned. If you abide in me and my words remain in you, ask whatever you will and it will be created for you. My Father's glory is evident as you produce a large crop of fruit and you grow more and more into becoming my disciples.

"I have loved you as the Father has loved me. Remain in my love. As you obey my commands you remain in my love, just as I obey my Father's commands and remain in his love. This I have told you in order that my joy may remain in you and that your joy may be completely full. My command is that you love one another as I have loved you. No one can have or demonstrate greater love than if you lay down your life for your friends. You are my friends if you do what I command. I don't call you servants any longer because a servant does not know what the master is doing. Instead I call you friends because I have revealed everything to you that I learned from my Father. You did not choose me, but I chose you and appointed you to go and produce a crop of fruit that will last. So the Father will give you whatever you ask in my name. Here is my command: Love each other.

"If the world hates you, just know that it first hated me. If you belonged to the world it would love you as its own dear friend. But you do not belong to this world. I have chosen you out of the world. Because of this the world hates you.

"Remember the things I told you: 'The servant is not greater than the master.' If they persecuted me, they will also persecute you. If they followed my teaching, they will also follow yours. All of this comes because of my name, and because they do not know the one who sent me. They would not bear the guilt of sin if I had not come to them and spoken. But now they have no cloak for their sin. Anyone who hates me also hates my Father. If I had not done things in their presence that no one else ever did, they would have no guilt. They have seen, and yet they have hated both me and my Father. But they fulfill what is written in their Law: 'They hated me without a reason.'

"When the Counselor has come, whom I will send to you from the Father—the Spirit of truth who proceeds from the Father—he will give witness about me. And you also are witnesses because, from the very beginning, you have been with me.

"I have told you all this so that you will not be turned away from me in shock. They will bar you from their gatherings for worship. The time will even come when those who kill you will think they are doing a favor for God. They will do these kinds of things because they have known neither the Father nor me. I am telling you this now so that when the time comes you will remember that I warned you about all of this. In the beginning I did not tell you about this because I was with you; but now I am leaving to go to him who sent me. None of you asks me, 'Where are you going?' because you are filled with grief since I have told you these things. But pay attention because I am truly telling you, things come together to your advantage because I go away. If I did not go away, the Counselor would not come to you. But when I go I will send him to you. He will come and he will demonstrate the world to be wrong about sin, and righteousness, and judgment. Wrong about sin, because people do not believe in me; wrong about righteousness, because I am going to the Father where you will no longer see me; and wrong about judgment, because the ruler of this world now stands condemned.

"I still have many more things to tell you, but the weight of it all is more than you have the capacity to carry right now. But when the Spirit of truth comes, he will guide you into the full truth because he will speak not on his own, but rather he will speak what he hears, and tell you what is coming. This will glorify me because from me he will receive what he reveals to you. Everything that the Father has is mine. That is why I told you the Spirit will take what is mine and will make it known to you."

"You will no longer see me in a little while. Then after a little while you will see me."

Some of his disciples asked each other, "What is he telling us when he says, 'You will no longer see me in a little while. Then after a little while you will see me,' and 'I am going to the Father'?" They kept on going, asking, "What does he mean by 'a little while'? We can't tell what he is saying."

Jesus knew that they wanted to ask him, so he said, "Are you wondering about my meaning when I said, 'You will no longer see me in a little while. Then after a little while you will see me?' I am telling you the truth. You will cry and grieve while the world is overjoyed. You will mourn, but your mourning will turn into joy. A woman in labor has pain giving birth to her child because the moment has arrived. But when her child is born she doesn't remember the anguish any longer because of her joy that a new baby has been born into the world. In that way you will have grief now, but I will see you and your hearts will rejoice, and no one will take your joy away from you.

"And when that day comes you will no longer request anything from me. Truly I tell you, my Father will give in my name whatever you ask. You have not asked for anything in my name up to this point. Ask and receive, so that your joy may be complete.

"I have been telling you these things with somewhat veiled words. An hour is coming when I will no longer use these kinds of figures but will tell you about my Father in plain words. On that day you will ask in my name. I am not at all saying that I will ask the Father for you. No! Because the Father himself loves you. He loves you because you have loved me and have believed that I come from God. I went from the Father and came into the world. And so now I leave the world and go to the Father."

His disciples said, "There! Now you are telling us these things without veiled figures. Now we know that you understand everything. We do not need to ask you more questions. By this we believe that you came from God."

"Do you really believe?" Jesus replied. "The hour is fast approaching when each of you will be scattered to your own home. And me you will leave all alone. You will all scatter and leave me on this very night. As it is written:

"'I will strike the shepherd,
>   and the sheep of the flock will be scattered.'

Yet I am not alone, for my Father is with me. And after I have risen from death, I will go ahead of you to Galilee."

"I have told you all of this so that in me you may have peace. You will have affliction in this world. But be hopeful. I have conquered the world."

And, having made this declaration, Jesus lifted his vision toward heaven and said, "Father, the hour is here. Glorify your Son, in order that your Son may glorify you, since you gave him rightful authority over all humanity so that he might give eternal life to all those you have given him. This, then, is eternal life: to know you, the one true God, and to know Jesus Christ, the one you sent. I glorified you on earth. I completed the work you gave me to do. So now glorify me together with you, Father, with the glory I had with you before the world was created.

"I have made your name known to the ones you gave me from the world. They were yours. You gave them to me and they have kept your word. Now they know that all the things you've given to me come from you, because the words you gave me I gave to them, and they accepted those words. They truly know that I came from you and they believe that you sent me. I ask for them—not for the world—but for those you have given me I am making my request because they are yours, and all I have is yours, and everything you have is mine, and I have been glorified in them. And I will no longer remain in the world. But they are still in the world, while I am coming to you. And so, Holy Father, protect them in the power of your name, the name that you gave me, in order that they may be one just as we are one. I protected them while I was with them. By the name you gave me I guarded them. And none was lost except the son of destruction, so that what was written is fulfilled.

"But now I am coming to you. I speak these things in this world, so that they may have my joy complete within them. I have given your word to them and the world has hated them because they are not of this world, just as I do not belong in this world. I am not praying and asking that you take them out of the world but that you protect them from the evil one. They no more belong to this world than I belong to it. Set them apart by the truth. Your word is truth. Just as you sent me into the world, I also have sent them into the world. For them I am sanctified so that they also may truly be sanctified.

"Not for them alone do I make this request. My prayer is also for those who will believe in me through their words, Father, that all may be one, just as you are in me and I am in you, that they also may be in us so that the world may believe that I am sent by you. The glory that you gave me I have given them, in order that they may be one just as we are one—I in them and you in me—brought to complete unity. Then may the world know that you sent me and that you have loved them even as you have loved me.

"Father, I long for all those you have given me to be with me where I am, and to see my glory that you have given me because you loved me before the creation of the world.

"I rightly call you Father, but the world has not known you. I knew you, and these have known that you sent me. I have made your name known to them, and will continue to make you known in order that the love you have for me may be in them and that I may be in them."

Prayer In The Garden

Matthew 26:36-46
Mark 14:32-42
Luke 22:39-46
John 18:1

Jesus now crossed the Wadi Kidron and his disciples went with him. On the other side there was a garden called Gethsemane on the Mount of Olives, and he and his disciples went into it.

And Jesus said to them, "Sit here and pray that you won't come under temptation, while I go over there and pray."

He took Peter and the two sons of Zebedee, James and John, along with him, and he began to grieve and to be deeply distressed. Then he said to them, "My soul is overwhelmed with sorrow to the point of death. Stay here and keep watch with me."

Going about a stone's throw away, he fell with his face to the ground and asked that, if possible, this hour might pass him by. "Abba, Father, you can do everything. May this cup be taken from me. Yet not as I want, but as you will."

An angel from heaven then appeared to him, strengthening him. He continued praying even more earnestly. And drops of his sweat fell to the ground like drops of blood.

He got up from prayer, returned to his disciples and found them sleeping, exhausted by their grief. "Why are you sleeping? Could all of you not keep watch with me for one hour?" he asked Peter. "Get up! Watch, and pray so that you won't come under temptation. The spirit is certainly willing but the body is weak."

Going away a second time he again prayed, "My Father, if this cup cannot be taken away unless I drink it, let your will be done."

Again he found them sleeping when he returned because their eyes were heavy. So leaving them, he went away once more and prayed a third time, the same as before.

He then came to the disciples and said to them, "Sleep now and rest. The hour is now arriving for the Son of Man to be betrayed into the hands of sinners. Look! Get up. Let's go! Here comes my betrayer!"

The Arrest

Now the one betraying him, that is Judas, also knew this place because Jesus often gathered with his disciples there. So Judas approached leading a band of soldiers and some officials from the chief priests and

Matthew 26:52-54
Mark 14:43-52
Luke 22:47-53
John 18:2-12

the Pharisees with lamps, lanterns, and armed with swords and clubs.

The one betraying him had set up a signal: "Whoever I kiss is the one; apprehend him and take him away securely."

Right away Judas came up to Jesus and said, "Rabbi!" and kissed him.

But Jesus said, "Judas, would you use a kiss to betray the Son of Man?"

Knowing all that was going to happen to him, Jesus asked them, "Who do you want?"

They answered him, "Jesus the Nazarene."

Jesus said to them, "I am."

Now Judas the betrayer stood right there with them. When Jesus said, "I am," they pulled back and fell on the ground.

He asked them again, "Who do you want?"

And they answered, "Jesus the Nazarene."

Jesus answered, "I said to you, 'I am.' So since you are looking for me, allow these others to go."

These words he had spoken were fulfilled in this: "I lost none of those you gave me."

The men laid hands on Jesus and seized him.

Simon Peter had a sword. He drew it and struck the slave of the high priest, and cut off his right ear. The name of the slave was Malchus.

Jesus told Peter, "Put your sword into its sheath! Father has given me this cup. Shall I not drink it? All who draw a sword will die by a sword. Or do you think I don't have the power to ask my Father to provide me at once with more than twelve legions of angels? But then how would the Scriptures be fulfilled that say it must be this way?"

And touching the ear, he cured him.

Then the detachment of soldiers, with its commander and the Jewish officials, bound Jesus.

And Jesus said, "As if I am a robber you have come out with swords and clubs to arrest me? I was with you daily in the temple courts teaching, and you did not arrest me. But this is how the Scriptures are fulfilled. This is your hour and the authority of darkness."

Then everyone left him and ran away. Now there was this young man following Jesus, and he was wearing nothing but a linen garment. And they took hold of him, but he left his garment behind and ran away naked.

Jesus Is Made To Appear Before The Temple Leaders

First they brought Jesus to Annas, the father-in-law of Caiaphas, who was the high priest that year. Caiaphas was the one who had advised the Jews that it would be desirable that one man would die for the people.

Matthew 26:57
Mark 14:53
Luke 22:54
John 18:13-14

Peter Was Following

Now Simon Peter was following Jesus at a distance, along with another

Matthew 26:58
Mark 14:54
Luke 22:54
John 18:15-16

disciple. This disciple was known to the high priest so he entered with Jesus into the high priest's courtyard, while Peter stood outside at the door. So the other disciple, the one known to the high priest, came back, spoke to the servant woman who was on duty at the door, and brought Peter in.

Peter Denies Knowing Jesus

Matthew 26:69-70
Mark 14:67-68
Luke 22:57
John 18:17-18

It was cold, and the servants and officials stood around a fire they had kindled to keep warm. Peter also was standing with them, warming himself. When the servant woman saw Peter warming himself she looked closely at him. "You aren't one of the disciples of that Nazarene, Jesus, are you?" she asked Peter.

He denied it, saying, "I don't know him, woman."

Jesus Is Questioned

John 18:19-24
Matthew 26:55

Meanwhile, the high priest was questioning Jesus about his disciples and his teaching.

Jesus answered him, "I have spoken plainly to the world. I always taught in synagogues and in the temple, where all the Judeans come together. I spoke nothing in secret. So why question me? Ask the people who heard me. They know what I said."

When Jesus had said this, one of the attendants standing nearby slapped Jesus and said, "Is this how you answer the high priest?"

Jesus answered, "If I said something bad, explain to everyone what is wrong. But if I said something good, then why did you hit me?"

Annas then sent him to Caiaphas the high priest, still bound.

Peter Denies Knowing Jesus A Second Time

Simon Peter was still standing by the fire warming himself. When the servant woman saw him there, she said again to those standing around, "This is one of them."

Matthew 26:69
Mark 14:69
Luke 22:58
John 18:25

So they asked him, "You are with Jesus the Galilean too, aren't you?"

He denied it, saying, "I am not."

Peter Denies Knowing Jesus A Third Time

But one of the servants of the high priest, a relative of the man whose ear Peter had cut off, said, "Didn't I see you in the garden with him?"

Matthew 26:73-74
Mark 14:70
Luke 22:59-60
John 18:26-27

Again Peter denied it, "I swear, I don't know who you're talking about," and he went out into the entryway.

At that moment a rooster began to crow. Immediately the rooster crowed a second time. Then Peter remembered what Jesus had told him: "Before the rooster crows twice you will deny you know me three times."

Then he was overcome with bitter weeping.

Jesus Is Tried Before Caiaphas And The Other Leaders

Matthew 26:57-68
Mark 14:53, 55-65
Luke 22:63-71

At dawn those who had arrested Jesus took him before Caiaphas the high priest; and all the chief priests, the elders and the teachers of the law had assembled.

Now the chief priests and the whole Sanhedrin were looking for false evidence against Jesus so that they could put him to death. But they did not find any. Though many false witnesses came forward, their statements did not agree. Eventually two came forward and said, "We heard him say, 'I am able to destroy the temple of God made with human hands and build a temple not made with hands over the course of three days.'"

Yet even then their stories did not match one another.

Then the high priest arose and said to Jesus, "Don't you have an answer to the accusations that these men are bringing against you?"

But Jesus stayed silent and gave no answer.

Again the high priest asked him, "I place you under oath by the living God. Tell us. Are you the Messiah, the Son of the Blessed One?"

Jesus said, "I am. If I tell you, you do not believe me, and if I were to ask you a question, you would never answer. But I declare to all of you, from now on you will see the Son of Man sitting at the right hand of the Mighty One and coming on the clouds of heaven."

Then the high priest tore his clothes and said, "Now you have heard blasphemy! What is your decision?"

"He deserves death," they answered.

Then those who were holding him spit in his face. They blindfolded him and struck him with their fists, and said, "Prophesy for us, Christ! Who is it that hit you?"

And the guards took him and beat him. And they hurled many other insults at him.

Jesus Is Turned Over To Pilate

Then all of the chief priests and the elders of the people bound Jesus and they took him from Caiaphas to the *Praetorium*, the palace of the Roman governor. It was early morning, and to avoid ritual uncleanness they did not enter the *Praetorium*, because they wanted to be able to eat the Passover meal.

<small>Matthew 27:1-2
Mark 15:1
Luke 23:1</small>

Judas Responds

When Judas, who had betrayed him, saw that Jesus was condemned he was

<small>Matthew 27:3-10</small>

filled with regret and took back the thirty pieces of silver to the chief priests and the elders. And he said, "I have sinned. I betrayed an innocent man."

But they said, "What is that to us? You see to it."

So throwing down the silver pieces in the temple, Judas left. And he went away and hanged himself.

The chief priests picked up the silver pieces and said, "It is not in accordance with law to put these into the treasury since it is the price of blood."

They deliberated and agreed to use the money to buy the potter's field as a cemetery for foreigners. So because of this it has been called the Field of Blood to this day. Then what was spoken by Jeremiah the prophet was fulfilled: "They took the thirty silver pieces, his valuation set by the people of Israel, and they used them to buy the potter's field, as the Lord commanded me."

Pilate Asks What Charges Are Laid Against Jesus

Luke 23:1-4
John 18:29-32

Pilate came outside to the whole gathering and asked, "What accusations are you bringing against this man?"

They were beginning to accuse him, saying, "We discovered this man corrupting our people. He forbids payment of taxes to Caesar and says he is Christ, a king. If he were not doing bad things, we would not have brought him to you."

So Pilate said, "Take him yourselves and judge him according to your own law."

The Jews answered him, "But we are not authorized to kill anyone."

This answer was to fulfill what Jesus had spoken about the kind of death he would die.

Pilate Asks Jesus, "Are You A King?"

So Pilate went back inside the *Praetorium*, summoned Jesus and said, "Are you the king of the Judeans?"

Matthew 27:11-14
Mark 15:2-5
Luke 23:3
John 18:33-38a

"You have said so," answered Jesus.

But to the accusations by the chief priests and the elders, he gave no response. Then Pilate asked him, "Don't you hear the many witnesses against you? Aren't you going to answer? Listen to how many accusations there are!"

But Jesus said nothing in response, and Pilate was astonished.

Pilate Sends Jesus To Herod

Pilate again went out to the Judeans and announced to the chief priests and the crowd, "I can't find a single charge against this man."

Luke 23:4-7
John 18:38

But they were insistent. They said, "He incites people all over Judea with his teaching. He began in Galilee and has now come here."

Pilate heard this and inquired if the man was a Galilean. So when he learned that Jesus belonged to Herod's jurisdiction, he transferred him to Herod, who was also in Jerusalem during those days.

Herod Questions Jesus

Luke 23:8-12

So Herod was very happy when he saw Jesus. He had wanted to see Jesus for a long time because, from what he had heard, he hoped to see a miraculous sign of some sort take place. He questioned him about many things, but Jesus gave no answer. The chief priests and the teachers of the law were standing nearby accusing him loudly. Herod and his soldiers then treated him with scorn and mocked him. They dressed him in a magnificent robe and returned him to Pilate. Herod and Pilate became friends that day. They had been enemies before this.

Pilate Questions Jesus Again

John 18:33-38

Pilate then went back inside the *Praetorium*, called Jesus, and asked him, "Are you the king of the Judeans?"

Jesus asked, "Do you say that of yourself, or did others say this to you about me?"

Pilate answered, "Am I Judean? These are your own people. The chief priests delivered you to me. What have you done?"

Jesus answered, "My kingdom is not of this world. If my reign were of this world my supporters would fight that I might not to be handed over by the Judeans. But my kingdom is not from this place."

So Pilate said, "You are a king, then!"

Jesus answered, "You say that I am a king. I was born for one thing and came into the world for one thing: to witness to the truth. All who belong to the truth listen to me."

Pilate said to him, "What is truth?"

Pilate's Wife Warns Him About Jesus

While Pilate was seated for the tribunal, his wife sent him this message: "Under no circumstances have anything to do with that innocent man, because I have suffered tremendously today in a dream about him." *Matthew 27:19*

Pilate Declares Jesus Innocent

With this he went out again to the chief priests and the rulers, along with the crowd of people, and said to them, "You brought me this man as one who was corrupting people and I have examined him in your presence. I have found nothing with respect to your charges against him. Neither did Herod, because he sent him back to us. Surely you *Luke 23:13-16 John 18:38 b.*

can see he has done nothing to deserve death. I will punish him therefore, and then release him."

Release Of Barabbas

Matthew 27:15-23
Mark 15:6-14
Luke 23:17-23
John 18:39-40

Now at the festival it was the governor's custom to release a prisoner chosen by the crowd. At that time they were holding a well-known prisoner named Barabbas. Pilate said to them, "You have a custom that I release for you one prisoner at the time of Passover. Do you want me to release 'the king of the Jews'? Do you want me to release Barabbas, or do you want me to release Jesus who is called the Messiah?" Because he knew it was out of envy that they had delivered Jesus to him.

They shouted back, "No! Give us Barabbas!"

Now Barabbas was a robber. But the chief priests and the elders persuaded the crowd to ask for Barabbas and to have Jesus put to death.

Pilate asked, "Then what will I do with Jesus who is called Christ?"

They all answered, "Crucify him!"

"For what? What evil has he done?" asked Pilate.

But the crowd shouted all the more, "Crucify him!"

Pilate saw that he wasn't getting anywhere, but that instead a riot was beginning. He took water and washed his hands in front of the crowd and said, "I am innocent of this man's blood. See how this is your doing!"

The whole crowd answered, "His blood be upon us and upon our children!"

Then Pilate released Barabbas.

Jesus Is Scourged And Crowned With Thorns

So Pilate took Jesus and had him lashed with a whip. The guards then led Jesus into an interior courtyard of the *Praetorium* and called together the entire troop of soldiers. They stripped his clothes off of him and placed a purple robe around his shoulders. They braided a crown of thorns and placed it on his head and put a staff in his right hand. Falling on their knees, they began to mock-praise him with, "Hail, king of the Jews!"

<small>Matthew 27:28-31
Mark 15:16-20
John 19:1-3</small>

They spit on him, and took the staff and beat him on the head. They slapped him.

Jesus Is Presented Again To The Crowd; Pilate Condemns Jesus

Pilate came out again and said to the crowd, "Listen! I am bringing him outside to you so that you will know that I found no substantial charges against him."

<small>Matthew 27:26
Luke 23:25
Mark 15:15
John 19:4-15</small>

Jesus came outside wearing the thorn crown and the purple robe, and Pilate said, "Here is the man!"

When the chief priests and their attendants saw him, they shouted, "Crucify! Crucify!"

But Pilate said to them, "Take him and crucify him yourselves. But as for me, I have found no substantial charge against him."

But the Judeans insisted, "We have a law, and according to that law he deserves death, because he claimed he was the Son of God."

So when Pilate heard these words he grew even more afraid. He went inside the *Praetorium* again and asked Jesus, "Where do you come from?"

But Jesus didn't give him an answer. So Pilate said, "Do you refuse to speak even to me? Do you not understand? I have authority to set you free and I have authority to crucify you."

Jesus answered, "You would not have power over me at all if it were not given to you from above. So the one who handed me over to you has greater sin than you."

At this Pilate searched for a way to set Jesus free, but the Judeans called out, "If you release this man you are not a friend of Caesar. Anyone who makes himself out to be a king speaks against Caesar."

So then, when Pilate heard these words, he brought Jesus out and sat down in the tribunal seat at the place known as the Stone Pavement but in Aramaic is called *Gabbatha*. Now it was before noon on the day of preparation for the Passover. "Here is your king," Pilate said to the Judeans.

But they called out, "Take him! Take him! Crucify him!"

"Your king? Crucify your king?" Pilate asked.

The Last Day Of The Earthly Life Of Jesus

The chief priests answered, "We have no king but Caesar."

So Pilate handed Jesus over to be crucified.

Jesus Carries The Cross

So the soldiers took Jesus. After they had mocked him, they stripped off the purple robe and put his own clothes back on him. Carrying the cross himself, he went out toward the place of the Skull, which is called Golgotha in Aramaic.

Matthew 27:31 b.
Mark 15:20 b., 23:26 a.
John 19:17 a.

Simon Of Cyrene Is Compelled To Carry The Cross

As they went out of the city gate they met a man from Cyrene, named Simon, who was passing by on his way in from the country. Simon was the father of Alexander and Rufus. They put the cross on him and forced him to carry it behind Jesus.

Matthew 27:32
Mark 15:21
Luke 23:26

Jesus Speaks To Those Who Are Following Him

Now following him there was a large number of people, including women who loudly mourned and wailed for him. But Jesus turned and said to them, "Daughters of Jerusalem, do not weep

Luke 23:27-32

for me, but weep for yourselves and for your children, because certainly the days are coming when it will be said,
> 'Childless women are the ones who are blessed;
> the wombs that did not give birth
> and the breasts that never nursed!'

Then
> " 'they will begin to say to the mountains, "Fall on us!"
> and to the hills, "Cover us!"'"

Because if they do these things when the sap is in the tree, what will happen when it is dry?"

Two others, who were criminals, were being led to be crucified with him.

Jesus Arrives At The Place of Execution

Matthew 27:33
Mark 15:22
Luke 23:33 a.
John 19:17 b.

They brought Jesus to the place called Golgotha, which means "The Place of the Skull."

Jesus Is Offered Wine To Drink

Matthew 27:34
Mark 15:23

They offered Jesus wine to drink, mixed with something bitter. And he tasted it but he did not drink it.

Jesus Is Crucified

Matthew 27:35 a.
Mark 15:24 a.
Luke 23:33
John 19:18

There they crucified him.

The Last Day Of The Earthly Life Of Jesus

The Soldiers Divide His Clothing

And Jesus said, "Father, forgive them, for they don't know what they are doing."

Matthew 27:35-36
Mark 15:24 b.
Luke 23:34 b.

When they had nailed him to the cross they took his clothes and divided them into four shares, one for each of them, with the tunic held out. They distributed his clothes among themselves by chance, casting lots to determine what each one would get. The tunic was woven in one piece from top to bottom, without seams. "Let's not tear it," they said to themselves. "Let's cast a lot for whose it will be."

This happened in order to fulfill the scripture:
> "They divided my garments among them,
> and cast lots for my clothing."

Then they sat down and they kept watch over him. It was before noon when they crucified him.

A Written Sign Of The Charges Is Placed Over His Head

Pilate had a notice prepared and fastened to the cross above his head with the written charge against him. And the notice of the charge read: "Jesus of Nazareth, the king of the Judeans." Many Judeans read this sign because the place where Jesus was crucified was near the city, and it was written in Aramaic, Latin

Matthew 27:37
Mark 15:25-26
Luke 23:38
John 19:19-22

and Greek. That led to a protest by the Judean chief priests. They said to Pilate, "Do not write 'The King of the Jews.' But instead write that this man claimed to be king of the Jews."

"What I have written is written," Pilate answered.

Jesus Speaks To His Mother And To The Beloved Disciple

John 19:25-27

Near the cross of Jesus stood his mother, his mother's sister, Mary the wife of Clopas, and Mary Magdalene. So when Jesus saw his mother standing nearby and one disciple whom he loved next to her, he said to his mother, "Woman, here is your son." Then to the disciple, "Here is your mother."

From that very hour this disciple took her into his home.

Jesus Speaks To The Two Criminals

Matthew 27:38
Mark 15:27-28, 32 b.
Luke 23:39-43
John 19:18

And with him they crucified two robbers, one on his right and one on his left, with Jesus in between.

Then one of the criminals hanging there jeered at him: "You're the Messiah, aren't you? Save yourself and us!"

But the other criminal answered him with a reprimand. "Don't you fear God, since you received the same sentence? It is right for us to be punished because we are getting back what our actions deserve. But this man did nothing wrong."

Then he said, "Jesus, remember me when you come into your kingdom."

And Jesus told him, "I promise you, today you will be with me in paradise."

Insults To Jesus

And also some who passed by jeered at him, shaking their heads, they said, "This one who was going to destroy the temple and in three days build it! Save yourself! If you really are the Son of God, come down from the cross!"

Matthew 27:39-43
Mark 15:29-32
Luke 23:36-37

And likewise the chief priests, the teachers of the law and the elders were ridiculing him. They said, "He saved others, but he isn't able to save himself! Some king of Israel he is! Now would be a good time for us to see this "Christ," this "King of Israel," come down from the cross, if we are supposed to believe."

" 'He trusts in God. Let God rescue him now if he wills it.'

"Didn't he say, 'I am the Son of God?'"

And the chief priests and scribes ridiculed him to one another, "He saved others, but he can't save himself!"

The soldiers also approached him and ridiculed him. They offered him bitter wine and they said, "If you are the king of Judea save yourself!"

Down The Last Road

Darkness Covers The Land

Matthew 27:45
Mark 15:33
Luke 23:44-45 a.

Darkness came over the whole land at around noon, until three in the afternoon, because the sun's light deserted the land.

Jesus Cries Out To God

Matthew 27:46-47
Mark 15:34-35

Then at about three in the afternoon, Jesus cried out in a loud voice, "*Eloi, Eloi, l'ma sabachthani?*"

That means, "My God, my God, why have you forsaken me?"

Upon hearing this, some of those standing nearby said, "Listen, this man is calling Elijah."

Jesus Is Offered A Sponge Full Of Bitter Wine

Matthew 27:48-49
Mark 15:36
John 19:28-29

Someone ran and got a sponge. He filled it with bitter wine, put it on a pole, and offered it to Jesus to drink. But the rest said, "Wait. Leave him alone. Let's see if Elijah comes to save him."

After this, when he knew that everything had now been completed, in order to fulfill the Scripture, Jesus said, "I thirst."

A container full of bitter wine lay there, so they took a soaked sponge of the bitter wine wrapped around a bunch hyssop stalks, and brought it to his mouth.

The Last Breath Of Jesus

When he had taken the bitter wine, Jesus said, "It is completed."
And Jesus called with a loud voice, "Father, into your hands I entrust my spirit."
With that he bowed his head, and gave up his spirit, and he breathed his last.

Matthew 27:50
Mark 15:37-38
Luke 23:46
John 19:30

Torn Open

And look! The curtain of the temple was torn in two from top to bottom. The earth quaked, the rocks split, and the tombs were opened. Many bodies of saints who slept were awakened and they came out of the tombs after the resurrection of Jesus and went into the holy city and showed themselves to many people.

Matthew 27:51-53
Mark 15:38
Luke 23:45

Reaction To The Death of Jesus

When the centurion guarding Jesus and those who were with him saw the earthquake and all the things that had happened, and saw how he died, they were terrified. The centurion praised God, then said, "Surely this man was innocent. In truth, he was the Son of God!"

Matthew 27:54
Mark 15:39
Luke 23:47-48

When the entire crowd who had gathered to see all of this experienced the unfolding of these events, they pounded their chests and went away.

The Women Who Followed Jesus Were Looking On

Matthew 27:55-56
Mark 15:40-41
Luke 23:49

But all those who knew him, including the women who had followed Jesus from Galilee serving him, stood at a distance watching what happened. Among them were Mary Magdalene, Mary the mother of James the younger and Joseph, the mother of Zebedee's sons, and Salome. Many other women who had come up to Jerusalem with him were also there.

The Side Of Jesus Is Pierced

John 19:31-37

Now the Judean leaders did not want the bodies left on the crosses during the Sabbath. Since it was the day of Preparation for the next day, especially because this was to be a special Sabbath, they asked Pilate to have the legs of the crucified men broken and their bodies taken down. So the soldiers came and broke the legs of the first one, and then those of the other who had been crucified with Jesus. But they found Jesus already dead when they came to him so they did not break his legs. But one of the soldiers pierced his side with a spear and a flow of blood and water came out right away. The one who saw these things has given witness, and his testimony is true. And concerning these things he knows that he speaks the truth, so you too may believe. For this happened in order that the scripture would be fulfilled. "His bones will not be broken," and, as another scripture says, "They will look on the one they pierced."

Jesus Is Taken Down From The Cross

As evening approached, there came a rich man from Arimathea, named Joseph. He went boldly to Pilate and made a request for permission to remove the body of Jesus. Joseph was a disciple of Jesus, but secretly because he was afraid of the Judean leaders. Joseph was a member of the Council of some stature, who was waiting with hope for the kingdom of God. He was a good and just man, who had not given his consent to the determination or action of the Council. (Matthew 27:57-58, Mark 15:42-45, Luke 23:50-52, John 19:38-39)

Pilate wondered if Jesus was already dead. He called the centurion and questioned him as to whether Jesus had already died. And when he learned from the centurion that Jesus was dead, Pilate gave the order for the body to be released to Joseph. So he came and removed the body. And Nicodemus came also, the one who had first visited Jesus at night. He brought a mixture of myrrh and aloes weighing around seventy-five pounds.

Down The Last Road

The Body Of Jesus Is Prepared For Burial

Matthew 27:59
Mark 15:46
Luke 23:53
John 19:40

Joseph took the body, and the two of them wrapped it in a clean linen cloth with the aromatic spices in the ordinary way the Judeans prepare for burial.

Jesus Is Laid In A Tomb And A Stone Is Rolled Across The Entrance

Matthew 27:60-61
Mark 15:46 b.-47
Luke 23:53 b.-56
John 19:41-42

Now there was a garden at the place where Jesus was crucified. And in the garden was a new tomb, in which no body had ever been laid. Since the tomb was nearby, and because it was the Jewish day of Preparation, Joseph placed Jesus in his own new tomb that he had cut out of the rock.

Now the women who followed Jesus from Galilee came along following Joseph. They saw the tomb and how his body was placed into it. Joseph rolled a great stone in front of the door to the tomb and went away. Mary Magdalene and Mary the mother of Joseph were sitting there opposite the tomb and saw where his body was laid. Then they returned to where they were staying and prepared aromatic spices and myrrh. And they observed the Sabbath by resting, obeying the commandment.

4

Study Notes

Study Notes

With this narrative now presented in a simple form, two questions and motivations give rise to this chapter of notes. The first question is, *how were the Gospels blended to create this one unified text?* These notes provide a way to quickly trace the episodes and look up the various reports as they contributed to the blended form. At the same time I have wondered how I might share this journey of discovery with anyone who is intrigued by the amazing unity of these four Gospels. In other words, *how might the whole of the story give rise to study of the day itself?* I have kept extensive notes from my research and I offer these notes as a way to engage in deeper study of the wonder of this day.

A critical approach to these texts might highlight elements that seem inconsistent with one another in the various accounts. In contrast, this blended translation is a deliberate attempt to interweave the reports without altering what any one writer says, without discounting any voice, and without presupposing what took place. While that might seem complicated or difficult, it turned out to be possible. The texts seemed to sort themselves as long as I held onto my original goal.

And yet, the specific order of events and dialogue is certainly a matter of judgment. The question constantly on my mind was, *How can I place these texts in an order that makes sense?* I resolved to do so without adding anything or leaving anything out. The final outcome represents an order that makes the narrative sequence flow naturally.

One key element in this process involved maintaining constant awareness of the physical location where each episode took place. While most of the narrative is carried by dialogue and action, the real order of the narrative is maintained by the location sequence.

This in itself is a remarkable confirmation of the essential unity of these four narratives. One way to visualize this underlying unity would be through the use of a map of Jerusalem and its surroundings in the time of Jesus. Make four copies of the map. Take the Gospel of Matthew and, without lifting your pen, draw a line representing the location of Jesus during the last 24 hours of his life as reported by Matthew. Then repeat that exercise for each of the other Gospels. The result is four maps that have almost exactly the same line.[7]

In other words, all four Gospels substantially agree about where Jesus was in each hour of a tumultuous 24 hour period. The only slight variation might be noted in Luke's report that Jesus was taken for trial before Herod and then promptly sent back to Pilate, while the other three Gospels don't mention any appearance by Jesus before Herod. Since very little of substance happens in Luke's *Herod episode*, it would be easy to see why the

---

[7] See, for example, *The MacMillan Bible Atlas* (map 236), which presents the entire path of Jesus in those last 24 hours without any notes as to variations in the basic locations of each event.

other Gospel writers might simply omit that part without comment.[8]

> ... we will not say that the diversity which we perceive in the three Evangelists was the object of express arrangement, but as they intended to give an honest narrative of what they knew to be certain and undoubted, each followed that method which he reckoned best.
>
> John Calvin *Harmony of Matthew, Mark, and Luke*

This highlights the divergence/congruity dynamic at work in these four Gospels. While a first reaction to variations between Gospels might be to judge some parts as inconsistently reported, the rubric of consistent/inconsistent or compatible/incompatible inherently involves making personal judgments that go beyond available evidence. It is much more helpful to think in terms of divergence or congruence with regard to these variations. Making note of when the texts diverge or are congruent places more focus on the actual words of the writers rather than on our judgments.

---

[8]In his discussion of Luke's report on the trial before Herod, I. Howard Marshall concludes, "... the origin of the story is hard to explain on any other hypothesis than that it reflects a historical episode told in the Lucan manner..." *Commentary on Luke*, 855.

Down The Last Road

If the writers were copying one another or sharing a common source the texts would most likely diverge less. We would wonder why any divergences occur at all. If they were completely independent of one another we would wonder why they are so congruent. If anything, my study of the text of the four Gospels shows they are congruent enough to demonstrate that they are reporting on the same basic events that happened in a defined 24 hour period. But they diverge from one another enough to suggest that while they may have made use of some common sources, their origins are mostly independent of one another. The congruence of the reports is best demonstrated by the overall outline of the day as it unfolds in locations agreed upon by all four writers.

So making note of the congruence of locations, with the substance of each event fixed, and with the natural boundaries of sequence and time assumed, the only remaining challenge (and the area that represented the greatest amount of individual judgment) was to place the actions and dialogue of each scene in a plausible order.

The box on the following page lists the location sequence of where Jesus was during his last 24 hours. The narrative includes reports of action and dialogue that took place in other locations as well. For example, it is reported that Judas went to meet with temple officials in the temple precinct. But the list of locations is where Jesus was during all of those 24 hours, and his location is key to understanding the order of events and coordinating the narratives of the four Gospel writers.

Study Notes

LOCATIONS

The narrative proceeds through a definite sequence and the locations of each episode can be used to cluster the action and dialogue along the path. The settings for each segment are as follows:

Upper Room

The Road from the Upper Room to the Garden of Gethsemane

In The Garden of Gethsemane

The House of Annas

The *Praetorium* or House of the Roman Governor

The Palace of Herod

Return to the *Praetorium* or House of the Roman Governor

The Road from the *Praetorium* to Golgotha, the place of execution

Golgotha, the place of execution

The Tomb

With those segments established, the following is a detailed look at the flow of narrative within each sequence. At key points I have included some approximate times of day using our current system of marking time. These are no more than my speculation about the timeline of that day, but I believe these estimates help to demonstrate the natural coherence in the sequence and flow of events as reported by the four Gospel writers.

Segment 1
Last Meal With Friends

Matthew 26:17–30, Mark 14:12–26,
Luke 22:7–38, John 13:1–14:31

Physical location: An upper room in Jerusalem

A great deal of study has been devoted to explaining the apparent difference between the three synoptic Gospel writers and John when it comes to identifying when the last supper took place relative to the Passover meal.[9] While I understand the complexity of this discussion, clarity emerges through

---

[9] See I. Howard Marshall, *Last Supper and Lord's Supper* for a thorough presentation of the problem and some suggestions for a solution.

simply believing the reports of all four writers and blending their accounts without trying to correct anything or obscure any seemingly contradictory details.

This is not to suggest that comparative research and critical study of the problems associated with the timing of the last supper are unimportant—only that those concerns faded as I pursued the goal of presenting the narrations in a composite form.

Preparations For The Evening Meal
Matthew 26:17–19, Mark 14:12–16, Luke 22:7–13

3 PM
Thursday

Order in the blended narrative:
Luke 22:7-11, Matthew 26:18,
             Luke 22:11-13

Location: The dialogue between Jesus and his disciples takes place outside of Jerusalem. His instructions lead them to go into Jerusalem.

This scene and dialogue serves as a sort of prelude to the last day, and is not actually part of the last day, which began at sunset. It was included to give readers a sense of the setting.

But from another standpoint this event may represent the beginning of the last *24 hours* of the life of Jesus. Jesus died a few hours before sunset on the next day. So the time when he sent the disciples to prepare the last meal may coincide with the time of day when he died 24 hours later. There is no clear time indication in any of the three Gospels as to when this conversation took place. This time estimate may be more symbolic on my part. The action of preparing for the last supper initiates the final sequence of the events of his life.

6 PM

Thursday
Sunset marks the beginning of the last day.

Reclining At The Table
Matthew 26:20, John 13:1–17

Location: A large upper room in Jerusalem.

John reports the washing of feet at the beginning of the meal. This is a case of one Gospel witness providing detail that others do not.

7 PM

Bread And Cup
Luke 22:15-20, Matthew 26:26-29, Mark 14:22-25,
I Corinthians 11:23-25

Order in the blended narrative: Luke 22:15, Luke 22:16, Matthew 26:26–28, Luke 22:20, I Corinthians 11:25

What did Jesus say when he offered the bread and cup to his disciples? A common answer to that question is a blend of all four Gospels with some of Paul's words in 1 Corinthians 11 stirred in. We know these words from their setting in communion liturgy, where it is typical to take parts of all four Gospels and some of 1 Corinthians 11:25 to make a smooth and complete blend.

At first I tried to create this segment without borrowing from Paul's statement in 1 Corinthians 11 at all. But then I considered how likely it is that Paul's account of the words of Jesus were committed to paper at an earlier date than any of the Gospels. Further reinforcement for the authenticity of Paul's quotation of Jesus is supplied in the reasoning of Dom Gregory Dix in his study of the liturgy.

> The most important thing which S. Paul says is that he believes that his 'tradition' about the last supper in I Cor. xi. comes ultimately 'from the Lord.' He must, therefore, in the nature of things, have supposed that at some point it passed through that primal group of Galilean disciples who formed the nucleus of the Jerusalem church, and who had been in any case the only actual eye-witnesses of what occurred at the last supper. He had himself only intermittent but direct contact with some of these men, and was in a position to check for himself their acquaintance with the story as he had received it.[10]

Embedded in these considerations is a relatively significant set of textual variants in Luke 22:17-20. In this case the variations are numerous and fairly complex. The section in question is the last part of verse 19 and all of verse 20. A

---

[10] Gregory Dix, *The Shape Of The Liturgy*, 63.

significant number of manuscripts omit those parts. As Metzger writes,

> Since the words in verses 19b and 20 are suspiciously similar to Paul's words in 1 Cor 11.24b-25, it appears that the latter passage was the source of their interpolation into the longer text.[11]

In other words, those who copied the Gospel of Luke appear to have added in the additional words that Paul had included in his letter to the Corinthian church.

However that may be, my initial decision to include everything without redundancy led to the final text. This may be regarded as a decision to include the longer version of Luke, or to incorporate 1 Corinthians 11:24-25.

The Gospel Of John And The Lord's Supper

Many have noted that John omits what we generally call "the Eucharist" or "the institution of the Lord's Supper" in his Gospel. It does seem odd that the Gospel of John does not report the giving of the bread and cup by Jesus to his disciples.[12] Interpreters have found it difficult to explain John's silence on the matter, but it is worthwhile to note that it is just

---

[11] Metzger, *Textual Commentary*, 176.

[12] It is frequently noted that the sayings in John 6, especially at 6:35, 51-58, are a close parallel with the words of Jesus about the bread and the cup as reported in the other Gospels. See H.D.A. Major, "Incidents In The Life of Jesus," in *The Mission and Message of Jesus*, 170. See also Aland, *Synopsis Of The Four Gospels*, 284.

Study Notes

that: silence.[13] From the beginning my purpose has been to piece together all of the reports without redundancy and without omission. The resulting narrative works fairly well and thus achieves my original goal. But perhaps it also smooths over some dislocations that would be worthy of further study. This particular problem serves to reinforce the need for using this blended text as a meditational guide only, and not as a primary form of the scriptures.

Throughout the reporting of the evening meal the order of dialogue and events becomes somewhat challenging. Each Gospel reports a similar general set of conversations that take place at the table, or on the way to the garden of Gethsemane. But the details of who was present when (Judas leaves part of the way through) and the exact order of when certain things were said is elusive. The order presented here is, again, governed by the original goal of the project. Everything is included without redundancy, nothing is altered, and the actions and dialogue are placed in an order so as to present a flowing narrative.

---

[13] Interpreters also note that some indications in the Gospel of John suggest that this meal took place the day before Passover (note John 19:24). See Marshall, *Last Supper and Lord's Supper*, 57.

Down The Last Road

9 PM

Jesus Predicts The Betrayal
Matthew 26:21-24, Mark 14:18-21,
Luke 22:21-23 John 13:21-30

Order in the blended narrative: Matthew 26:21, John 13:21–22, Matthew 26:22, John 13:23–25, Matthew 16:23–24, John 13:26–30

When does Judas leave the group in order to go and guide those who are dispatched to arrest Jesus? Matthew, Mark, and Luke report that Jesus identified Judas as the betrayer. But none of them tell us when Judas slipped away.

Intriguingly, John does report when Judas slips away (John 13:30). But he also notes that when Judas left it was not seen as a significant event by any of the disciples at the time (John 13:28–29). It is almost as though John knew the other Gospel writers omitted what seems like a significant detail. And yet, we cannot assume that John had the other Gospels in front of him when he recorded these events. Several factors indicate that he did not. This is one of several inadvertent confirmations of the veracity of these reports. John is telling us that no one seemed to notice when Judas left, and the other three independent reports inadvertently confirm that by not even mentioning the event when it took place. They simply reported when Judas showed up again in the garden, having never really noticed when he left.

Study Notes

Jesus Predicts Simon Peter Will Deny Him

Matthew 26:31–35, Mark 14:30–31, Luke 22:31–34, John 13:31–38

Order in the blended narrative: John 13:31-36, Luke 22:31-34, Mark 14:30-31

Some difficulty in placing this part of the narrative within the whole arises. I have placed it here according to the order in the Gospel of Luke.

In the blended narrative a few instances occur when dialogue is set in one segment or location in contradiction to where it is set in one or more of the Gospels. The Gospel of John, with Luke's concurrence, reports that Jesus predicted the denial of Peter while they were around the table in the upper room. Matthew and Mark report this same prediction but the setting is on the way to Gethsemane. I have placed this dialogue in the setting of the upper room. There is no strong reason for this decision, since the Gospel writers are split on this decision 2-2.

Because the betrayal by Judas is also discussed at the table, placing the dialogue regarding Peter's denial tends to lead toward comparison and contrast. Such comparison and contrast is natural regardless of where this conversation took place so again, the setting does not seem extremely important to the narrative–only that it took place sometime during the meal or before prayer in the garden.

9:30 PM

A Dispute About Who Is Greatest
Luke 22:24-30

Luke is the only Gospel that places this conversation around the table of the last supper. A critical approach might cast doubt that this conversation occurred in this setting. But following the plan to include everything, the dialogue is placed here, following Luke's order, suggesting that it took place after the bread and cup.

What Is Needed For This New Mission
Luke 22:35–38

Luke presents this conversation as the last word before Jesus and his disciples departed for prayer in the garden. Because the narration of the next set of events is brief in the Gospel of Luke, the immediacy of connection between these words of Jesus about a sword and his arrest is very apparent. This points to a shortcoming in the blended narrative. Each Gospel writer juxtaposes dialogue and events for important reasons. By inserting the following section from the Gospel of John I have woven the two narratives together, meeting my original goal of telling everything that happened in the most natural order. But it must be noted that something is also lost in this effort.

On the other hand, Luke's narrative creates a sense of immediate connection between the words of Jesus about a sword and the use of a sword in an attempt to prevent the arrest. That immediacy creates a narrative highlight, but in all practicality the walk from the upper room to the garden, and the time of prayer before the soldiers arrive, is significant. So by placing Luke's narrative in the flow of what the other Gospel writers have included, a certain effect is achieved. The resulting flow of narrative is more true to how things took place in real time. This highlights the advantage of reading the Gospel stories together.

Jesus Teaches The Disciples At The Table
John 14:1–31

A Passover meal may easily take three or four hours. But the descriptions given in Matthew, Mark, and Luke of what happened can be read in a couple of minutes. Clearly much more was said at the table, and John fills in some of what that was.

Note that John clearly marks the point when the group gets up from the table and begins to walk to the garden. (John 14:31) This transition is noted even though the teaching of Jesus naturally continues without any strong sense of transition in John chapter 15. The Gospel of John is sometimes spare in its description of the material elements in an episode. But when objects are noted or when a geographical location is indicated, the reason for including the description is usually meaningful.

> ## Segment 2
> ## From Upper Room To Prayer In The Garden
>
> Matthew 26:36–46, Mark 14:32–42, Luke 22:39–46, John 14:39 b.–18:1

10 PM — Departing From The Upper Room

Luke 22:39, John 14:31b.

Order in the blended narrative: John 14:31b., Luke 22:39

Sunset takes place around 6 PM in Jerusalem in early spring. A typical Passover seder lasts about four hours. So it seems fitting to estimate that Jesus and his disciples left the upper room at around 10 p.m.

Luke notes that going to the Mount of Olives "was his custom," (Luke 22:39) and John later states that the reason why Judas knew he could find Jesus there is from previous experience (John 18:2).

Study Notes

Teaching Along The Way From The Upper Room To The Wadi Kidron

Matthew 26:31-32, John 15:1-17:26

10:00 PM to 10:45 PM

Physical location: The road from the upper room to the garden of Gethsemane.

Order in the blended narrative: John 15:1–16:32, Matthew 26:31–32, John 16:33–17:26

Jesus took his disciples through the streets of Jerusalem and then out of the city. They went down into the Kidron valley and then climbed part way up the Mount of Olives until they reached Gethsemane. Along the way he spoke to them. It is helpful to consider that the Temple would have been prominently visible during part of their walk. Night would have obscured some things, but the Temple would have been well lit. Jesus had been warning them not to put their trust in the ponderous strength of the Temple. He had warned that, though it seemed eternal, it would in fact be torn down soon. The words of Jesus in these chapters of John should be read in the context of the visual presence of the Temple as Jesus spoke.

As reported by Josephus, a prominent feature of the Temple decoration was a vine, ". . . from which clusters of grapes hung as tall as a man's height."[14] It seems that John wanted the reader to know the location of where these words were spoken so that the visual impact might be apparent.

---

[14] Josephus Flavius, *The Wars of the Jews*, V 5: 4, translated by William Whiston.

Study Notes

Segment 3
Prayer In The Garden And The Arrest

Matthew 26:36-56, Mark 14:32-52, Luke 22:39-53, John 18:1-12

Prayer
Matthew 26:36-46, Mark 14:32-42, Luke 22:39-46, John 18:1

Order in the blended narrative: John 18:1, Matthew 26:36, Luke 22:40, Matthew 26:36–38, Luke 22:41, Matthew 26:39, Mark 14:35, Luke 22:43–46, Mark 14:38, Matthew 26:42–46

Physical location: A garden on the Mount of Olives called *Gethsemane*.

A well-known variation exists in Luke 22:43-44, which I chose to include.

11 PM

Luke 22:43 An angel from heaven then appeared to him, strengthening him. Luke 22:44 He continued praying even more earnestly. And drops of his sweat fell to the ground like drops of blood.

Study Bibles generally note that some ancient manuscripts do not include verses 43 and 44 of Luke chapter 22. So should these verses be included? Dr. Bruce Metzger casts significant doubt on the inclusion of these verses in the original manuscript in Luke based on a survey of the evidence available. His *Textual Commentary On The Greek New Testament* was produced as the result of the work of a committee of scholars who weighed in on each passage in question. The nature of the manuscript evidence led to a negative assessment on whether these verses were in Luke's original manuscript. And yet he concludes his discussion by writing,

> Nevertheless, while acknowledging that the passage is a later addition to the text, in view of its evident antiquity and its importance in the textual tradition, a majority of the Committee decided to retain the words in the text but to enclose them within double square brackets.[15]

I included these verses knowing full well that some doubt is associated with them. While I am not qualified to overrule the scholars who came to a different conclusion, my view of the whole narrative leads me more toward their inclusion rather than dismissing them as a later addition.

---

[15] Metzger, *Textual Commentary*, 177.

Study Notes

The Arrest

Matthew 26:52-54, Mark 14:43-52, Luke 22:47-53 John 18:2-12

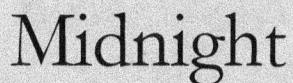

Order in the blended narrative: John 18:2-3, Mark 14:44-45, Luke 22:48, John 18:4-9, Mark 14:46, John 18:10-11 Matthew 26:52-54, Luke 22:51, John 18:12, Mark 14:48-49, Luke 22:53, Mark 14:50-52

The specific details of the narratives on the arrest scene do present a first impression of conflicting statements. By placing all of the narratives together as I have done, the conflict disappears somewhat. Matthew and Mark both relate that Judas kissed Jesus as a sign to the crowd of which person to arrest. In John there is no mention of a kiss and Jesus identifies himself before Judas has any opportunity to begin his task. Luke's account is something of a mediation (Luke 22:47-48). In the blended version of the story a somewhat more complicated narrative emerges, as compared with any of the Gospels by itself. If we remind ourselves that it was nighttime in an era with no artificial light, and the scene being narrated unfolds very rapidly, then the sense of confusion and conflict over whether Judas actually kissed Jesus or not seems accurate to the way things probably unfolded.

"I Am" in John 18:5

My translation of one phrase from the Gospel of John in this section is extremely literal. Confronted with a detachment of soldiers, Jesus asks them to tell him who it is they are looking for.

> John 18:5 They answered him, "Jesus the Nazarene."
> Jesus said to them, "I am."

The phrase, "I am," runs against the grammar of the type of answer we would expect in English. All of the translations I consulted modified the phrase from the literal translation to make Jesus's answer sound like better English with the exception of *The Complete Jewish Bible*, which translates the phrase literally as I do. Some use various notation methods to indicate that their translation differs from the literal.

While I value the choice to present the Bible in standard English, and while it seems almost like an evasion of the question the way Jesus literally answers, this is one instance where I believe the literal translation is essential to understanding what Jesus said. Jesus was referring back to Exodus 3:14 and other passages where the name of God is given as a form of *I Am* in Hebrew.[16]

The soldiers reacted to these two words by drawing back and falling to the ground (John 18:6). This reaction would not make any sense unless they were responding to the power of his deity. No soldiers fall back and hit the ground when they simply

---

[16] Morris, *The Gospel According to John*, 473-474, 743.

Study Notes

learn that the one they are supposed to apprehend is standing calmly right in front of them.

Interpreters who are working with an English translation of this passage which translates the response of Jesus as "I am *he*," tend to seek ways of altering the response in 18:6 by altering the underlying Greek without any manuscript evidence.[17] It is worth translating the phrase literally, even though the outcome is somewhat awkward in English, for the sake of expressing the force of the underlying Greek text.

---

[17] See, for example, Wright, *Jesus: The Revelation of God*, in *The Mission and Message of Jesus*, 910.

Segment 4
Trials

Matthew 26:57-27:26, Mark 14:53-15:15, Luke 22:54-23:25, John 18:13-19:16

3 AM Friday — Jesus Is Made To Appear Before the Temple Leaders

Matthew 26:57, Mark 14:53, Luke 22:54, John 18:13-14

Passage used in the blended narrative: John 18:13-14

Segment 4 has been broken down into small sections in order to correlate events from the Gospels accurately. While the underlying events are the same, the Gospel writers tend to use their own unique wording in the descriptions. This opening event is a good example. A simple thing takes place. Jesus is taken to the house of the high priest to be questioned. I would expect that the wording for such a simple event would be similar in all four Gospels. How many different ways are there to say it? And why not copy the wording verbatim from some source if it was available? And yet, for this simple event, the wording varies greatly, while all four Gospels generally say the same thing. My brief survey of commentaries did not uncover any explanation of this, perhaps because the variations of wording do not affect anything that seems important to the main story. But these variations do point to more underlying independence of these four narratives than is generally acknowledged.

Some difficulty arises in trying to accommodate all four Gospels with regard to who was present to question Jesus in the initial trials. Hoskyns points to the problem when he writes,

> The record of an examination before Annas and the obscure reference to further examination before Caiaphas (v. 24) present considerable difficulties, since the synoptic narrative records only one Jewish trial, which Matthew explicitly states to have been before Caiaphas.[18]

Note how the blended translation of all four Gospels entirely obscures this problem. By simply including all reports in a plausible sequence the apparent conflict disappears. This is not to suggest that there is no apparent conflict, only that the problem is of an abundance of detail, more than a problem of contradictory reporting. I have concluded that all four Gospels record the basic scenes of these 24 hours, but each writer adds

---

[18] Hoskyns, *The Fourth Gospel*, 511-512.

some description of some events that did not make it into the accounts of any other of the writers.

I used the Gospel of John for this opening description because it has the greatest amount of specific detail.

Peter Was Following
Matthew 26:58, Mark 14:54, Luke 22:54, John 18:15-16

Order in the blended narrative: John 18:15–16

While the Gospel of John gives more detail, all of the Gospel writers moved to the reporting of the denial of Peter right after they noted that Jesus was being questioned. This seems to be happening simultaneously with the questioning of Jesus. Various narrative techniques may be used by writers to depict simultaneous action—cutting back and forth between scenes that are happening at the same time, or narrating one entire scene and then narrating the other with some indication that the action was happening at the same time. The differences between the Gospels on the order can be ascribed to these differing narrative strategies. In the end, my decisions of ordering this sequence were simply an effort to honor the differing strategies of the Gospel writers and still present a coherent narrative.

Study Notes

Peter Denies Knowing Jesus
Mark 14:67-68, Luke 22:57, John 18:17-18

Order in the blended narrative: John 18:18, Mark 14:67, John 18:17, Mark 14:68, Luke 22:57

Physical location: The courtyard of the high priest.

While it is difficult to match all of the details of all of the Gospels precisely with regard to how and when Peter was confronted as a follower of Jesus, a remarkable similarity in the accounts does stand. This portion of the story tested my ability to carry out my original purpose of including everything stated in all of the Gospels. But the basic narrative line holds. All four Gospels report that while Jesus was being questioned, Peter was nearby and he was also questioned. While Jesus was holding onto his integrity with those who were questioning him, Peter was failing.

Jesus Is Questioned
John 18:19-24, Matthew 26:55

Order in the blended narrative: John 18:19–24

In order to encompass all of what is reported about the denial of Peter and the questioning of Jesus I chose to pause the series of denials and report the questioning by Annas as per the Gospel of John, and then pick up the narrative thread of

Peter's denial later. This seemed to preserve the best order from the standpoint of the reader who is considering events that happened simultaneously.

Peter Denies Knowing Jesus A Second Time

Matthew 26:69, Mark 14:69, Luke 22:58, John 18:25

Order in the blended narrative: John 18:25, Mark14:69, John 18:25, Matthew 26:69

All agree that Peter was challenged three times, and three times he failed. The details of each challenge don't easily align.

Peter Denies Knowing Jesus A Third Time

Matthew 26:73-74, Mark 14:70, Luke 22:59-60, John 18:26-27

Order in the blended narrative: John 18:26 –27, Mark 14:71, John 18:27, Mark 14:72

Again, the goal of natural narrative flow has driven the selection of details.

Study Notes

Jesus Tried Before Caiaphas And The Other Leaders
Matthew 26:57-68, Mark 14:53, 55-65, Luke 22:63-71

Order in the blended narrative: Matthew 26:57, Mark 14:53, Luke 22:66, Matthew 26:59–60, Mark 14:56, Matthew 26:61, Mark 14:58–59, Matthew 26:62–63, Mark 14:61, Matthew 26:63, Mark 14:62, Luke 22:67–68, Matthew 26:64–67, Mark 14:65, Luke 22:65

By placing all the the pieces of this narrative together in an order that sounds natural the general feel of the trial emerges.

The Trials Of Jesus Before Pilate and Herod
Matthew 27:1-26, Mark 15:1-20, Luke 23:1-25, John 18:28-19:16

6 AM to 10 AM

Order in the blended narrative: See the individual scene segments below for the order of each scene.

All time indicators point to an early morning trial. The rooster has crowed, and Pilate is available to hear the charges. It seems like about four hours go by with the various interactions. We know that Jesus was on the cross by noon (Matthew 27:45, Mark 15:33, Luke 23:44-45 a.).

Jesus Is Turned Over To Pilate
Matthew 27:1-2, Mark 15:1,
Luke 23:1, John 18:28

Order in the blended narrative: Matthew 27:2, John 18:28

Judas Responds
Matthew 27:3-10

Matthew alone reports the remorse of Judas. This remorse is directly a result of the condemnation of Jesus by the chief priests. That element of the response of Judas would be obscured if his remorse came at any other time in the narrative.

This illustrates something about the flow of events. Everything must be placed according to the internal logic of each Gospel.

It should be noted that this action could have taken place simultaneously with some of what follows. We know that some of the temple officials went to the the *Praetorium* for the trial before Pilate. But the leaders mentioned here could be some who were attending in the Temple. There would have been enough temple officials to have some at each location.

Study Notes

Pilate Comes Out And Asks What Charges Are Laid Against Jesus
Luke 23:1-4 and John 18:29-32

Order in the blended narrative: John 18:29, Luke 23:2, John 18:30–32

John included this somewhat formal request by Pilate for a definite statement of charges. Of course we would expect such a statement, and it seems to be implied in the other Gospels. This is one more instance where the flow of the narrative makes more sense to the contemporary reader when all of the accounts are blended together.

Pilate Asks Jesus, "Are You A King?"
Matthew 27:11-14, Mark 15:2-5, Luke 23:3, John 18:33-38a

Order in the blended narrative: John 18:33, Luke 23:3, Matthew 27:12–13, Mark 15:4–5, Matthew 27:14

This question, reported in very similar ways in all four Gospels, forms the crux of the accusation against Jesus. The ironic sign placed on the cross (John 19:19) reinforces this accusation as the primary charge against him. And yet the question, "Why was Jesus executed?" is not so easily answered. Reading all of the Gospels together provokes considerable thought about that question, which may be one of the most valuable reasons for doing so.

Down The Last Road

Pilate Sends Jesus To Herod
Luke 23:4-7, John 18:38

Order in the blended narrative: John 18:38, Luke 23:5–7

The trial before Pilate is broken into segments because Luke reports that Pilate sent Jesus to be tried by Herod part way through. According to Luke's narrative, Herod failed to deliver any verdict and sent Jesus back to Pilate. That may have led the other Gospel writers to consider the questioning by Herod to be insignificant. Luke may have understood that while Herod did not condemn Jesus, he did not release Jesus either. Given that Pilate had put the trial into Herod's hands, it would have been possible for Herod to do justice by letting Jesus go. Luke may have sensed the significance of passive consent.

Even though the Gospel of John does not mention sending Jesus to be tried by Herod, this is the point in that Gospel that expresses the exasperation of Pilate with the whole proceeding. So from that standpoint it seemed like a natural place to cut to the report of Luke.

Herod Questions Jesus
Luke 23:8-12

This scene is reported only by Luke. Luke seems to regard it as significant that Pilate and Herod became friends on this day, and the other Gospel writers may not have seen that fact as significant enough to report.

Study Notes

Pilate Questions Jesus Again
John 18:33-38

The Gospel of John reports the trial from the perspective of one who has entered the interior of Pilate's court. So some of the details seem to come from additional questioning in a less public setting.

Pilate's Wife Warns Him About Jesus
Matthew 27:19

This one verse in Matthew reports an event not mentioned in any of the other Gospels.

Pilate Declares Jesus Innocent
Luke 23:13–16, John 18:38 b.

Order in the blended narrative: John 18:38b, Luke 23:13–16

This overt declaration of innocence is only reported in Luke and in John.

Ironically, this declaration of the innocence of Jesus is all the more condemning of Pilate in the final outcome. Because he knew Jesus was innocent, he labored intensively to find a way to let him go. Nothing happened to change the facts before him regarding the supposed crimes of Jesus. But in the end he condemned Jesus to death.

Because a blending of all the reports of the four Gospel writers brings out a multitude of ironies like this one, the net effect is to see that *everyone* is responsible for Jesus's death. It is not as though the guilt can be divided into such tiny fractions so as to partially exonerate the many small actors in this scene. Each person's guilt unfolds in such a way as to make it complete and inexcusable. And yet, hidden within the complete condemnation rests the hope of redemption. Jesus reveals our need of his death in the very way he died, while also revealing the hope of his atoning grace.

Release of Barabbas
Matthew 27:15-23, Mark 15:6-14, Luke 23:17-23
John 18:39-40

Order in the blended narrative: Matthew 27:15-17 b., John 18:39, Matthew 27:18, John 18:40, Matthew 27:20, 22-26 a.

This event is reported in all four Gospels in varying degrees of detail.

The name "Barabbas" has given rise to a good deal of contemplation. The name is Aramaic and probably means "son of a father."[19] It is difficult to imagine how that could be a name, since it literally applies to half of all human beings. The

---

[19] Plummer, *Matthew*, 389.

nature of this name has given rise to some speculation. Interpreters have suggested[20] a symbolic meaning.

Amid discussions regarding the name "Barabbas," some manuscripts read "Jesus Barabbas," both in Matthew 27:16 and 27:17. This would suggest that "Barabbas" was a patronymic, and that the given name of this prisoner was "Jesus." Since "Jesus" (Hebrew "Yeshua") was a fairly common name it is not unreasonable to suggest that this prisoner known as "Barabbas" may have had the full name "Jesus Barabbas."[21] The evidence for and against this reading in the ancient manuscripts suggests that it is unlikely that the prisoner's name truly was "Jesus Barabbas," though that is how a few ancient manuscripts read.[22]

My translation included both names initially. At first I was swayed by the reasoning that it seems unlikely for some scribe to randomly assign the name "Jesus" as the given name of "Barabbas." In other words, it is hard to explain how the name "Jesus" was added in some manuscripts. It seems more likely that scribes were offended by the suggestion that a murderer could have the same given name as Jesus, and so the prisoner's first name was dropped during the making of copies at some point.

In the end I still feel that it makes great symbolic sense that Jesus the Messiah, who was innocent, would die in the place of Jesus Barabbas, the guilty murderer. It makes symbolic

---

[20] Just, *Luke*, 355.

[21] See Stern, *Complete Jewish Bible*, Matthew 27:16

[22] Metzger, *Textual Commentary*, 67-68.

sense that the Son of the Father would die for a son of a father, (and daughters of mothers too!) But it is too jarring for readers to cope with the name "Jesus Barabbas." I felt I could not leave that reading without distracting everyone.

Jesus Is Scourged And Crowned With Thorns
Matthew 27:28-31, Mark 15:16-20, John 19:1-3

Order in the blended narrative: John 19:1, Mark15:16, Matthew 27:28–29, Mark15:18–19, John 19:3

Matthew and Mark report this event as occurring after Pilate delivered Jesus to be crucified. John reports the same scene but shows Pilate still seeking a way to release Jesus after the scourging. By following the order of the Gospel of John, I was attempting to present the flow of narrative most compatible with all of the reports.

Jesus Is Presented Again To The Crowd
Pilate Condemns Jesus
Matthew 27:26, Luke 23:25 b., Mark 15:15, John 19:4-15

Order in the blended narrative: John 19:4-15, Mark 15:15

A difficult incongruity relates to the time of day for the trial and crucifixion. Did the crucifixion happen at the "third hour" or at the "sixth hour." This problem has been noticed since the time of the early church and several theological and symbolic

Study Notes

explanations have been offered. Saint Augustine resolved it this way:

> One Evangelist says that the Lord was crucified at the sixth hour, and another at the third hour. Unless we understand it, we are left wondering. When the sixth hour was already beginning, Pilate is said to have sat on the judgment seat. In reality when the Lord was lifted up upon the tree, it was the sixth hour . . . They had killed him already at the time when they were crying out. The government officials at the sixth hour crucified, the transgressors of the law at the third hour cried out. That which some did with hands at the sixth hour, others did with tongue at the third hour. More guilty are they that with crying out were raging, that they that in obedience were serving.[23]

This explanation is not completely satisfactory as it makes a theological point out of something that seems undoubtedly to be a flaw.

After experimenting with several alternatives I concluded that the most faithful translation of the phrases "about the third hour" and "about the sixth hour," is the same: "before noon." We need to remember that no one had a watch in the ancient world. Dawn was around 6 a.m. and so noon was about six hours after dawn. "The third hour," if calculated precisely, would be 9:00 a.m. But it is anachronistic to demand precision of this phrase. Likewise, "the sixth hour," if measured precisely,

---

[23] Saint Augustine, quoted from *Ancient Christian Commentary on Scripture*, New Testament II, *Mark*, 230.

would be from 11:00 a.m. to noon. To avoid interjecting interpretations of my own, and to avoid presenting a conflict where no true conflict exists, I translated both phrases as "before noon."

Study Notes

Segment 5
From the *Praetorium* to Golgotha

Matthew 27:31b.-32, Mark 15:20 b-21, Luke 23:26-32, John 19:16–17

This segment is short. It is marked off as a separate segment because it represents a different physical location than the one preceding it and the one following it.

Jesus Is led Out To Be Crucified

Matthew 27:31 b., Mark 15:20 b., 23:26 a., John 19:17 a.

10 AM

Order in the blended narrative: John 19:16, Mark 15:20, John 19:17

See the notes under the next section.

Simon Of Cyrene Is Compelled To Carry The Cross
Matthew 27:32, Mark 15:21, Luke 23:26

Down The Last Road

Order in the blended narrative: Matthew 27:32, Luke 23:26 Mark 15:21, Luke 23:26

One area of seeming contradiction may be summarized by the question, *Did Jesus carry his own cross, or did the soldiers force Simon of Cyrene to carry it for him?*

The answer to this question is a good illustration of the process I followed generally. So, I am providing this detailed explanation as a sample of the sort of thinking required to blend these texts together.

As can be seen in the blended narrative of that section, careful translation of passages, without inserting guesses of what is likely to have taken place, yields a relatively smooth and problem-free narrative.

As I originally approached this part of the narrative I did feel apprehensive about how I would make the narratives compatible for this part of the story. John seems to be emphatic that Jesus carried his own cross all of the way to Golgotha. Yet all three of the other Gospel writers agree that someone else was forced to carry it for him, and they all name the same person who did it: Simon of Cyrene. But here is where careful attention to exactly what each writer says, along with the aid of a map, and combined with the experience of walking that same route through Jerusalem, actually serves to reinforce the authenticity of these witnesses.

There is a fine line here. I did not want to translate and place things in order based on *what I thought must have happened*. And yet the statements of the Gospels needed to be placed in order. So instead of reconstructing or filling in to make the narrative smooth, I made every effort to simply answer the question, *What do the four Gospel writers think happened?*

A comparison between the account of Luke and the account of John on this point creates a sense of incompatibility. Luke's brevity makes it seem like Jesus never carried the cross at all, while John never notes that anyone but Jesus carried the cross. Mark and Matthew report that Jesus had already traveled some distance before Simon of Cyrene was pressed into service. Each of them include details that together show how this must have happened just outside the city gate. Now this is not at all obvious in a quick read of either the Matthew description or the details given by Mark. Read Matthew 27:31–32 and you will get the impression that the soldiers compelled Simon to carry the cross near the beginning of the route from the trial to the place of execution. Mark 15:20–21 adds a few more details but the casual reader would not likely question where this takes place. Without reading carefully it will seem like Simon of Cyrene is passing by the Fortress Antonia, the Roman *Praetorium*, when he is forced to carry the cross for Jesus. Except even a cursory glance at a map of Jerusalem from that period raises an immediate question: why would a non-Roman Judean casually pass by the Fortress Antonia? Especially at Passover, especially with all of the commotion, crowds shouting, soldiers on edge— what could possibly have been going through the mind of Simon of Cyrene to have placed him right outside the Fortress Antonia at that moment?

The answer to that question does not determine the placement of the narratives. It is more of a question that pushed me toward further research and a more cautious process of placement.

Those familiar with Jerusalem at the time would have intuitively understood that the meeting with Simon of Cyrene just would not have happened right outside of Pilate's Palace. The modern reader's assumption that Simon was compelled to carry the cross just outside of the *Praetorium* is false, as can be seen by carefully reading these verses from Matthew and Mark together. For the sake of those who read Greek I am going to print this in the original, but don't worry if you don't read Greek because I will explain what you are looking at in English.

Matthew 27:31-32 . . . καὶ ἀπήγαγον αὐτὸν εἰς τὸ σταυρῶσαι.

³² Ἐξερχόμενοι δὲ . . .

Matthew 27:31 ends with, literally, ". . . and they led him in the crucify." Then verse 32 says, "But as they came out . . ."
It would be stretching the Greek phrase εἰς τὸ σταυρῶσαι "in the crucify" too much to suggest that it might mean "towards the place of crucifixion." εἰς or "in" is a preposition with a variety of uses in Greek, but careful study suggests the best way to read this phrase is, "They led Jesus out *for the purpose* of crucifying."[24]

With that in mind we turn to Mark who says that Simon was "passing by on his way in from the country." Luke uses a

---

[24] Dana and Mantey, *A Manual Grammar of the Greek New Testament*, 104.

similar phrase. The most reasonable explanation for the use of this phrase is that Mark means for us to understand that this happened at the city gate. "On his way in" means that this happened as Simon entered the walled city of Jerusalem from out in the surrounding area. And a map of the time shows a substantial distance from the place where the trial and beating took place to the most likely gate where Jesus would have been forced to exit the city on his way to the place of execution. So now the phrasing chosen by Matthew makes a lot more sense. The literal translation of Matthew says the soldiers "led Jesus in the crucify," or "for the purpose of crucifying," meaning they marched him through the streets with his cross beam on his back. The Romans did not simply execute prisoners by crucifixion, they crucified in order to create terror. They paraded the condemned prisoner through the streets as a warning to everyone.

By the time Jesus got to the city gate the soldiers found it necessary to force the nearest passerby to carry the cross the rest of the way. Just at that moment Simon of Cyrene was, unfortunately, entering the gate and he was compelled to carry the cross the rest of the way.

But why didn't John make note of this? Why does he seem to insist that Jesus carried his cross the whole way, and why don't the other writers start by saying that Jesus carried his own cross out of the city? Here is where a map, a chance comment by Luke, and the personal experience of walking the streets of Jerusalem, explains everything. John reports the trial from the perspective of someone who has gained insider access to the events. John is saying that he watched Jesus leave the

Praetorium carrying his own cross. His is the perspective of one viewing the event from inside. Would John have followed along behind? He does not say that he did. If he were following, would he even have been close enough to Jesus to see someone else taking over the burden of carrying the cross? Coming from inside, as he would have been, it would have been difficult to follow closely behind because of the nature of crowds. If John wanted to go see what was to happen to Jesus, as we know from his later report that he did, he would have taken a different route to Golgotha. And every other route, according to the map of the time, is a good deal longer. He most likely would not have been present when Jesus arrived at the place of execution with Simon of Cyrene carrying his cross. John does not give any detailed report of Jesus arriving at the place of execution. He only reports that it happened (John 19:18). The sum is, any number of logistical reasons would explain why John never witnessed Simon of Cyrene carrying the cross.

But wouldn't he have heard the story later? Wouldn't he have added the detail about Simon of Cyrene carrying the cross? John never seems to report anything he can't verify himself, and he never seems to purposefully contradict the reports of the others. He simply writes what he knows to be true, and he is meticulous about that.

So what we have in this one small event is a set of reports that seem contradictory on the surface. At some early stage, in an effort to harmonize the accounts, any number of slight changes could have been made in the wording. But the church left the narratives as they were despite the problematic nature of the details. And a careful inspection shows how all of the little idiosyncrasies of the reports add up with one another to inadvertently verify the exact reports of all the others.

John 19:17 should be viewed as a summary narrative that leaves out some detail that is picked up by the other three.

Jesus Speaks To Those Who Are Following Him
Luke 23:27–32

Since Jesus was no longer carrying the cross he had the ability to speak to those who were following him. Luke is the only one who reports that Jesus spoke on the road toward crucifixion.

> # Segment 6
> # The Execution
>
> Matthew 27:33-50, Mark 15:22-37, Luke 23:33-46,
> John 19:18-30

Jesus Arrives At The Place Of Execution
Matthew 27:33, Mark 15:22,
Luke 23:33 a., John 19:17 b.

Passage used in the blended narrative: Mark 15:22

This is a simple description of the same event in all four Gospels. Yet the wording is different though they all say essentially the same thing.

Jesus Is Offered Wine To Drink
Matthew 27:34, Mark 15:23

Passage used in the blended narrative: Matthew 27:34

Only Matthew and Mark report the offer of a drink at this particular point.

Study Notes

Jesus Is Crucified
Matthew 27:35 a., Mark 15:24 a., Luke 23:33, John 19:18

Passage used in the blended narrative: Luke 23:33

It is interesting to note that while the English translation of the primary phrase in this passage, ". . . there they crucified him," is virtually identical in all four Gospels, none of them have the exact same phrasing in the underlying Greek. This is one of many examples of wording that indicates the writers of these documents weren't copying one another, nor were they copying directly from a common source. Yet they agree about what happened.

The Soldiers Divide His Clothing
Matthew 27:35-36, Mark 15:24 b., Luke 23:34 b., John 19:23-24

Order in the blended narrative: Luke 23:34, Matthew 27:35, John 19:23, Mark 15:24, John 19:23-24, Matthew 27:36, Mark 15:25

The verses are presented in this order to adequately include all of the detail offered in all four Gospels.

A Written Sign Of The Charges Is Placed Over His Head
Matthew 27:37, Mark 15:25-26, Luke 23:38, John 19:19-22

Down The Last Road

Order in the blended narrative: John 19:19, Matthew 27:37, Mark 15:26, John 19:20–22

In Luke 23:38 the Geneva Bible of 1599 includes a phrase that is unlikely to have been in the original manuscript of Luke. The unlikely phrase is about the languages posted on the cross over Jesus:

> "And a superscription was also written over him, in Greek letters, and in Latin, and in Hebrew, THIS IS THAT KING OF THE JEWS."[25]

The *King James Version* also included the phrase. Both of these translations were using what is known as the *Textus Receptus*, which was the best Greek edition of the New Testament in their day. But studies of the manuscripts show that it is very unlikely that the phrase about the languages, "in Greek letters, and in Latin, and in Hebrew," was in Luke's original manuscript. It is generally thought that a scribe who was copying Luke's Gospel added this based on what John's Gospel reported.[26]

In contrast with the doubtful nature of manuscripts for this phrase in Luke, the manuscripts for John 19:20 solidly support the conclusion that this phrase regarding the three languages belongs. Yet notice how the variant reading in Luke has no impact on my blended translation. Because the phrase

---

[25] Geneva Bible of 1599 from https://www.biblegateway.com

[26] Metzger, *A Textual Commentary*, 180-181, 253.

was already included from the Gospel of John, whether or not the phrase also appears in Luke's Gospel does not matter when we are trying to absorb the complete story from all of the Gospels.

All in all, the known manuscript variations do not substantially change the one story as it is told by the four Gospels.

Jesus Speaks To His Mother And To The Beloved Disciple
John 19:25-27

Some difficulty arises in trying to blend all the reports of what Jesus said on the cross. In the end I placed this report from John in a position prior to when darkness covered the land. That is, of course, a problem because the Gospel of John does not mention the darkness.

Jesus Speaks To The Two Criminals
Matthew 27:38, Mark 15:27-28, 32 b., Luke 23:39-43, John 19:18

Order in the blended narrative: Mark 15:27 John 19:18 Luke 23:39–43

Luke reports the details of Jesus's dialogue with the two criminals.

Insults To Jesus
Matthew 27:39-43, Mark 15:29-32, Luke 23:36-37

Order in the blended narrative: Matthew 27:39–42, Mark 15:32, Matthew 27:43, Mark 15:31, Luke 23:36–37

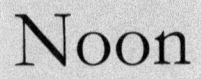

Darkness Covers the Land
Matthew 27:45, Mark 15:33, Luke 23:44-45 a.

Order in the blended narrative: Luke 23:44–45

Jesus Cries Out To God
Matthew 27:46-47, Mark 15:34-35

Order in the blended narrative: Matthew 27:46, Mark 15:34, Matthew 27:47, Mark 15:35

Jesus Is Offered A Sponge Full Of Bitter Wine
Matthew 27:48-49, Mark 15:36, John 19:28-29

Order in the blended narrative: Matthew 27: 48, Mark 15:36, Matthew 27: 49, John 19:28–29

Study Notes

The Last Breath Of Jesus
Matthew 27:50, Mark 15:37-38, Luke 23:46, John 19:30

3 PM

Order in the blended narrative: John 19:30, Luke 23:46, Matthew 27:50

> # Segment 7
> # After Jesus Dies
>
> Matthew 27:51-61, Mark 15:38-47, Luke 23:45-56, John 19:31-42

Torn Open
Matthew 27:51-53, Mark 15:38, Luke 23:45

Order in the blended narrative: Matthew 27:51-53

The observation about the torn curtain is mentioned in a different sequence in Luke as compared with Matthew and Mark. Luke groups the torn curtain together with the darkness, and the result is that the report of the torn curtain is just before the last breath of Jesus. Matthew and Mark do not report the torn curtain until after Jesus dies.

Reaction To The Death Of Jesus
Matthew 27:54, Mark 15:39, Luke 23:47–48

Order in the blended narrative: Matthew 27:54, Mark 15:39, Matthew 27:54, Luke 23:47, Matthew 27:54, Luke 23:48

Study Notes

The Women Who Followed Jesus Were Looking On — 4 PM

Matthew 27:55-56, Mark 15:40-41, Luke 23:49

Order in the blended narrative: Luke 23:49, Matthew 27:55, Luke 23:49, Matthew 27:56, Mark 15:40, Mark 15:41

The Side Of Jesus Is Pierced
John 19:31-37

This event is reported only by John. A close look at the sequence of events in the other three Gospels shows that there was plenty of time for this to take place, and good reasons for why this might only be witnessed by one who lingered at the place of execution after all of the other followers of Jesus had left.

Jesus Is Taken Down From The Cross
Matthew 27:57-58, Mark 15:42-45, Luke 23:50-52, John 19:38-39

Order in the blended narrative: Matthew 27:57, Mark 15:43, John 19:38, Mark 15:43, Luke 23:50–51, Mark 15:44–45, Matthew 27:58, John 19:39

Because all four Gospel writers add their own small details to the narration of this the resulting blend is quite rich in vivid description of what took place.

5 PM — The Body Of Jesus Is Prepared For Burial
Matthew 27:59, Mark 15:46, Luke 23:53
John 19:40

Order in the blended narrative: Matthew 27:59, John 19:40

Matthew, Mark, and Luke only mention Joseph of Arimathea in the burial preparation narrative. John adds that Nicodemus was also there. John also gives additional description about the preparation of the body.

6 PM — Jesus Is Laid In A Tomb And A Stone Is Rolled Across The Entrance.
Matthew 27:60-61, Mark 15:46 b.-47, Luke 23:53 b.-56, John 19:41-42

Order in the blended narrative: John 19:41–John 19:42, Matthew 27:60, Luke 23:55, Matthew 27:60–61, Mark 15:47, Matthew 27:61, Mark 15:47, Luke 23:56

Study Notes

Things That Happened Later

As with all narratives, it is difficult to know where to end the account. My sense of the events is that Jesus was laid in the tomb and the entrance was sealed just before sundown. The closing of the tomb feels like the end. But, of course, we know where these Gospel writers are going with their story. Matthew already has included a definite declaration of what is to come in 27:52-53. When Jesus died, the curtain of the Temple was torn, "and the tombs were opened. Many bodies of saints who slept were awakened and they came out of the tombs after the resurrection of Jesus and went into the holy city and showed themselves to many people."

So the ending presented by the closing of the tomb may only be considered an intermediate pause in a larger story. The 24 hours are over with the setting of the sun. The last day of the life of Jesus on earth is concluded when his body is sealed in a cave.

A few significant things take place between the burial and the resurrection. For example, Matthew reports that the next day after Jesus died a guard was placed at the tomb and the tomb was sealed (Matthew 27:62-66). While this is a crucial detail in the overall narrative, I decided to stay within the parameter of 24 hours.

The end of the story of that day is the beginning of a new chapter in the story of God's renewal of the world. My only motivation for dwelling on the story of this day is to point to the offer of new life presented to us when this day was consumed by the resurrection of Jesus.

5

Using This Resource

Using This Resource

I created this comprehensive narrative of the last 24 hours of the life of Jesus on earth so that people may easily read the one story that these four witnesses have written. This can be as simple as opening to the first page of chapter 2 and reading until you are through the story. In about 45 minutes the narrative can be easily read.

The Bible has a multitude of words to represent the human capacity for "knowing," "understanding," "considering," and so on. This represents the many ways that information is registered within us. With that in mind I have created the *Study Notes* chapter as a way of touching more on the analytical side of how this narrative is experienced. "Meditation" can imply a more experiential contemplation of the flow, without much critical thought involved. Or it may mean breaking things down into smaller pieces and thinking very seriously about how those pieces fit together and what they mean.

Some people absorb things better when they hear them. Some people have a hard time sitting still and will do better if some movement is involved. Some people listen better when they are in a group; others, when they are alone. Some have heard every part of this story so many times that the words wash over them without sticking. Breaking down the reading into smaller sections may help for some. There simply can be no singular "right way" to absorb this story. Without complicating the essential simplicity, thought should be given to the best way of taking in this story. This chapter is designed to help you find the way of taking this story that is best for you.

Here are some suggestions for how to let the experience of this story have a greater impact on your life.

Personal Devotional Use

Within your own pattern of daily prayer, you may choose to read this narrative from beginning to end in one sitting. If you ordinarily have a set time of prayer you might set aside that time on Good Friday to simply read the text through prayerfully. Also consider reading the narrative beginning around 2:30 in the afternoon on Good Friday as a way of matching the time of your reading with the actual event of Jesus's death. Consider going to a semi-darkened room in the afternoon and lighting a candle for reading. When you come to the end of the reading, blow out the candle and sit in the dark for a few moments and consider what it means that Jesus was willing to do all of that for you.

Family Use

In some ways this story may be too much for children, especially in its raw and complete form. And yet the impact of the death of Jesus is most powerful because Jesus exposes the dark, underlying evil of this world in the truest sense. Is it really possible that God could be born into the world, could lead a

Using This Resource

completely sinless life, could teach and heal and gather people into a new community, could exhort everyone to follow God's ways wholeheartedly, and the result would be that we would kill him for it? That is the essence of this story. It is harsh and frightening. Parents need to decide how to introduce children to the raw reality of this story with appropriate timing or else it could become a bad experience.

Yet at some point, perhaps when the children are in the teen years, parents may decide to read this story as a family to mark the significance of Good Friday. In our home the time after dinner was often the best time for family worship and learning experiences.

If you choose to do this, be sure and think rather carefully about the impact of this story on the outlook and mood of everyone who participates. Friday night is often a social night, so it may be disconcerting to have dinner, read this narrative, and then go off to some Friday evening entertainment as though nothing significant happened. You will want to plan for a way to process the feelings that might arise out of the narrative. Let family members share what meant the most to them, as well as what parts were troubling. The gloom of this story may be thick. Some of the power of it might linger for a time in the hopelessness that we experience as our personal influence and social structures can't fix the lurking violence and sin in the world. After all of these years the church is still too much like Judas the betrayer and Peter the denier. And yet leave time for anticipating the coming reality of the hope alive to us at Easter. Good Friday is not the last word. Be sure everyone leaves the experience looking forward to eternal life won for us in the resurrection of Jesus rather than being filled with the dread inherent in mocking trials, the lash, and the wounds of nails in hands and feet.

Congregational Use

Congregations often have a brief and simple Good Friday service. In my experience this is often a sparsely attended event and participation is awkward. It is difficult to know just how to mark the event of Jesus's death when the church spends so much time living in the hope of eternal life that springs from the resurrection. While we understand that the suffering of Jesus was necessary to take away our sin, the overwhelming reality of our complete salvation makes it confusing to understand what to do with the suffering of Jesus.

And yet the power of this story must never be too far away from the experience of the church. Jesus has brought us from death to life by throwing himself into the chaos of our world.

A congregation may want to gather at noon on Good Friday and simply read this story framed in prayer, worship, and song. Or, going further, a church that is eager to fully embrace the impact of these 24 hours may schedule a vigil to keep watch through all of these events. While it may not be practical to stay up all night reading each segment on the corresponding hour to when it occurred, it may not be asking too much to read this text as a community in three segments. In the context of a Maundy Thursday service the first part of the story could be read up to the arrest in the Garden of Gethsemane. In a Friday morning vigil, before everyone goes to work, the accounts of

Using This Resource

the trial could be read. And then at three in the afternoon the congregation could gather once more to hear the final portion of the story narrating the crucifixion, death, and burial. Those who can't be present for all three could still have a copy of the text and read each portion within the right time frame.

A Reading Plan For Maundy Thursday and Good Friday

Maundy Thursday and Good Friday are times for growing closer to Jesus by reflecting on what he was going through during those hours. By investing just a few minutes of your time you can read what the Gospels say about those events over the course of this day. This Reading Plan suggests dividing the reading into three time segments in order to place yourself in the middle of those events.

The Reading Plan divides the Simple Narrative into three segments: Thursday evening, Friday morning, and Friday afternoon.

However you choose to go through these events I trust that you will grow spiritually as the life of Christ is impressed upon your soul.

Reading Plan
Read through the blended account of the events in the life of Jesus during his last day in three segments.

Thursday evening: Read from the beginning of the story through the arrest of Jesus (pages 21 through the bottom of 37).

Down The Last Road

Friday morning: Read from when Jesus was made to appear before the temple leaders (the bottom of page 37) up through when Pilate delivers Jesus up to be crucified (the top of page 51).

Friday afternoon: Read from when Jesus carries the cross up through the end when Joseph and Nicodemus close the tomb. (from the middle of page 51 to the end on page 60).

Each of the Gospels presents the last day of the life of Jesus on earth as a significant prelude to the endless grace of the resurrection. As the events are unfolding, everything seems fraught with meaning. Death, betrayal, suffering, and hopelessness all seem to be the only meaning to be gathered from this dismal narrative of human depravity.

But then the resurrection entirely upends all of that. Each Gospel writer emphasizes various parts of what happened for important reasons. But now, with this blended narrative, you may begin to see the love of Jesus in a more complete way. Take some time to reflect on how this day in the life of Jesus conveys God's unchanging love for you.

Some Questions For Reflection

1. Do any details of the story stand out for you as you reflect on the blended narrative?
2. Which parts of the story are more vivid to you as a result of reading the whole story?

3. How is this story speaking into your life right now?
4. What next steps of discipleship are required by the events of those 24 hours?

As a Dramatic Reading on Maundy Thursday and Good Friday

Once the basic text of this narrative was created I began to think of ways to present it to people as part of the observance of Holy Week. If you are considering presenting this as a dramatic reading for a church or community you will want to order *The Last Day: Director's Script* (coming in 2022) in order to plan the presentation. Then when you know roughly how many readers will be involved you will want to order that number of copies of *The Last Day: Reader's Script*. The number of readers will vary based on local considerations, so you will want to have a preliminary plan before you order your copies of the *Reader's Script*.

The script is designed so that it can either be presented as a two Act play on one night, or as two separate plays on consecutive nights. Is it best to perform this whole script either on Maundy Thursday or Good Friday in one sitting? Or is it better to break up the story and perform the first half on Thursday and the second half on Good Friday? Obviously these are questions that need to be answered in conjunction with the pastor and others who might be planning the whole schedule of events for Holy Week. When this script was performed for the first time we presented the whole story, beginning to end, at a Good Friday service. A straight read-through of the whole thing takes about 45 minutes, so with music the service itself took just under an hour. That initial script was a bit longer than the final result presented in the current script because I included the whole text of the *Simple Narrative* verbatim. The current script has been shortened just slightly because some of the extended passages of Jesus speaking in the Gospel of John, while very important, are too long for most listeners to remain engaged.

It is possible to present the whole script on one night, Act I and Act II presented in a continuous reading with little or no break in between. The local needs and attendance patterns can dictate whether the one performance would come on Thursday or Friday. But it may be more effective to break the narrative into two parts, and the notes for how to do this are obvious within the script. Act I is for Maundy Thursday and Act II is for Good Friday. If you do it this way Thursday can include an extended time for celebrating communion within the reading of the script. Then at the moment when Jesus is arrested and his disciples abandon him the service comes to an end. The script picks back up the following night with the more somber tone of Good Friday. This lends itself more to a candlelight service of quiet reflection from which participants leave in silence.

Just reading? Or is there singing too?

As this was a worship service, we felt we wanted to include time for singing. Without breaks the extended reading sections are somewhat lengthy. Listeners may have a hard time paying attention for so long. So we would recommend

Using This Resource

incorporating congregational singing to break up the length of uninterrupted reading. Special music performances might also work.

All of this is designed to lead people into an experience of being with Jesus in his worst hours. Music has a way of drawing our spirits into the truth of this story. You may ask a few people to share with you which songs have made the love of Jesus on the cross must tangible for them. Consider how different people are moved in different ways. Some people are drawn into the story best when they are listening to talented musicians perform. Others will only be able to enter in when they are singing along. This diversity is always present when people are gathered for worship, but special services of worship bring an opportunity for fresh thinking on how to serve a wide variety of needs.

Good Friday and the Stations of the Cross

People have walked the same road that Jesus walked every Good Friday for many hundreds of years. "Stations" along that road mark the events of the first Good Friday. And all around the world the pattern of those stations in Jerusalem is emulated so that people may walk the sorrowful way without traveling to the Holy Land. Along the way, 14 events are traditionally commemorated. Fourteen stations mark specific events in that one day of the life of Christ. These are known as the 14 Stations of the Cross. They mark events from when Jesus was condemned to death until he was laid in the tomb. Some of these events are not taken from the Gospels, but instead come from later traditions associated with the events of Good Friday.

By starting with the entire text of *Down The Last Road* I have created a set of 14 stations similar to the stations in Jerusalem. This book is entitled, *Scenes From The Last Journey: 14 Points On The Way of the Cross*. The 14 events recounted in this book come directly from the pages of the four gospels. These are not identical with the traditional 14 stations, but rather these 14 points along the last journey of Jesus have been selected to reflect the Biblical accounts from the betrayal and arrest until Jesus is laid in the tomb.

This tells the story from beginning to end, but it doesn't tell the whole story. These 14 scenes have been selected out of the entire narrative.

As a follower of Jesus I have made an annual practice of returning to this story every year in preparation for Easter. The suggestions here are for how you could use this narrative every year to grow closer to the One who died so that you could live.

6

About This Translation

About This Translation

Any story has a much more significant impact when the audience pays attention to the unfolding of details from beginning to end, without interruption. I created this composite translation so that readers would be able to simply progress through everything the Bible says about these events without moving back and forth between the four Gospels. I have gone through the accounts of Matthew, Mark, Luke and John and spliced their actual words together into one unified narrative. Wherever there was complete overlap of an episode I chose the words of the Gospel writer who provided the greatest detail. I blended portions of one or more Gospels into the descriptions of others wherever it was necessary to complete the picture.

In a sermon on the Gospel of John, Chrysostom said,

> If a man cannot learn well a melody on pipe or harp, unless he in every way strain his attention, how shall one, who sits as a listener to sounds mystical, be able to hear with a careless soul?[27]

---

[27] Chrysostom, *Homilies*, 3.

Down The Last Road

I recognize the strain he describes. This blended translation records my effort to hear what we have been told about this day in the life of Jesus. While I did everything I could to filter out my own opinions and to present the narrative just as the four Gospels report the events, some decisions involving judgment were required in order to make it all work. In this chapter I will present my description of how I translated, blended, and ordered the narrative.

The composition of our four Gospels is a complicated mix of memories from four reporters of one series of events. Here is where the temptation to either critique or reconstruct emerges. It is tempting to filter the reports either through some theory of how each Gospel arose, or the theological concerns that appear to have driven their selection of events, or a reconstructed sense of the faith communities that treasured the earliest oral traditions. Or it may be tempting to flatten some of the variabilities for the sake of presenting a focused narrative for contemporary readers. These are precisely the leanings that tempted me. And yet I resolved to adopt a method that would eliminate these tendencies. To the best of my ability I have simply translated each Gospel's report of each episode and placed the translations into a coherent sequence.

So in order to fulfill this mandate I made a conscious effort to identify and lay aside my perceptions to simply let the reports speak for themselves. This was especially important in the instances of seeming inconsistency between Gospels. New Testament scholars regularly grapple with these. Most of the time my perceptions of inconsistency dissolved as I looked very carefully at the actual Greek texts. In some cases the appearance

About This Translation

of inconsistency was heightened in the English translations and differences seemed more like quibbles when the various meanings possible within the Greek were examined. In some cases the differences in reporting could easily be due to where the observer was standing in the crowd when the event took place. In some cases our perceptions of the customary practices of the day create the appearance of conflicting accounts. But a plain understanding of the texts, just as they are, presents a remarkably unified story of the events.

The process of translation for this project was inductive from the beginning, and characterized by a great number of inter-connected choices. Ordinarily a translator works with a defined text and renders that text into another language with accuracy and consistency, and along the lines of a particular linguistic style. While all of those aims were a part of this project, the nature of my particular goal necessarily required fluidity. While I was making translation decisions I was simultaneously comparing the variety in the reports, making judgments about order and redundancy, probing the manuscript evidence for the most reliable reading of each section, as well as considering other factors along the way. I constantly had to return to the primary goal: to create a composite translation of everything the Bible says about these events without omission or redundancy. Wherever there was complete overlap of scene I aimed for the greatest detail. I blended portions of one or more Gospels into the descriptions of others wherever it was necessary to complete the picture.

To some degree I developed my methodology of translation right while I was grappling with some of the many decisions. Only after I had been working and experimenting for a time, and only after much of the work of translation was completed did I take time to reflect on the rationale that was driving my method.

My goal has been achieved to the extent that I did not waver from the simple, foundational constraints of the project. I was tempted to stray from my own resolutions several times. The desire to resolve apparent conflicts by altering the story is intense. For those who are interested in the principles underlying this blended translation I am offering this brief description of my method.

The Greek Manuscripts

As part of the process of making this blended translation I needed to look at variations in the Greek manuscripts of these passages. In no case would any of the known variations substantially change my translation. But the translation is dependent upon certain decisions regarding the authentic Greek text of the Gospels.

Before beginning the process of translation we must first ask the question, what text are we translating? While it may cause some anxiety to know that any variation exists at all in the Greek text that translators use to publish the Bible, it should be a comfort to know that of the many thousands of copies of the New Testament that were made by hand over the nearly 1500 hundred years before the printing press, relatively little variation is present.

In most cases the few questionable variants in the manuscripts only add redundancies. For that reason they were

About This Translation

unimportant to the outcome of my project since I blended the accounts without redundancy.

As can be seen in the *References* section at the back of this book, I used four different publications of the Greek text of the New Testament to make this translation. These four sources should be regarded as a sort of safety net. They helped keep me from some potential mistakes. But in the end, the text of the New Testament is well-established and previous generations of scholars have duly noted all of the unlikely variants.

The text of my translation is based primarily on The Greek New Testament, Third Edition, published by the United Bible Societies, 1983, and the Greek Text of the Nestle-Aland 26th Edition. The *Textus Receptus*, was also consulted from time to time. I did also consult the First Edition of the Nestle text, but in light of the other editions this seemed superfluous.

For those who view progress as invariably positive it would seem superfluous to consult anything but the latest edition of the Greek text. I tend to take a more cautious approach. Most of the time the discoveries of one generation of scholars are built on the progress of those who came before. But sometimes a wrong turn is taken and then later conclusions falter. That is why I took the time to check with earlier editions of the Greek New Testament text and weighed the conclusions of later scholars against the earlier.

Process And Method Of Translation

As I began the process of creating a blended translation, I followed the axiom, *When in doubt, believe each writer.* In my experience, when four people have witnessed intense events and they are all telling the same story, they all have different observations to add. They all want you to know what it was like from their perspective. If they are in the same room telling their story they have a hard time keeping quiet while another is speaking. This is just how human beings feel when a story is being told that they have witnessed. Our four Gospel accounts are not exactly the same as when four people tell a story together that they all know. But the situation is like that in some ways. The Gospel writers appear not to have read each other's accounts. And when they were writing, of course, they were not all in the same room together. But by carefully arranging their accounts side by side we can hear each report in the context of the others.

So this blended account feels true to life with regard to the way people tell what they have seen and heard. The resulting blended narrative is full of dramatic dialogue and compelling events that flow in a way that matches our common experience of reality. A picture of the whole story emerges in this blended translation that feels complete and well-rounded. In other words, the process of reading all four Gospels together demonstrates that, together, they tell us everything we need to know about that day. None of the detail included is unnecessary.

But why did this need to be done by creating an original translation rather than simply splicing together portions from one of the many standard English translations available today?

Copyright restrictions made using one of the standard English translations impossible. But beyond that, it would not have been fair to the translators of those versions of the Bible

About This Translation

to take their work and use it that way. They made and published their translations for specific purposes and the dynamics of my project were not in view when they did so.

My goal was to create a highly accurate translation in a style that is easily readable in the English of our time. As with all translations created by a single translator, the result is a personal translation and therefore subject to the prejudices and perspectives I hold. Most likely, my translation is too literal at times, and too figurative at others. My only plea is that this is honestly how the Greek text of the Gospels reads to me.

In producing this blended translation I consciously intended to avoid inserting my own judgments whenever possible. This meant neither critiquing the Gospels nor shaping the material in any way. This does not mean I naively believed that I could escape the biases of my perspective, or that I believed I could simply wish away the parts of the story where it seems the writings of one seems incompatible with another. But rather it means I deliberately doubted my own sense of these events and resolved to place the reports given by these Gospels into the most natural sequence suggested by the events they report. I resolved to doubt my sense of conflict between the reports rather than doubt the reports themselves. I deliberately distrusted my sense of which reports are redundant and which reports are narrating separate events. I chose never to correct the reports by my research, but to believe the reports and look for ways that the research can support the accounts.

A good example of how I attempted to hold my suppositions in check might be found in the whole question of how to integrate the Gospel of John, which frequently contains material not found in the other three Gospels. My natural skepticism raised flags when integrating the reports of John into the narrative. But whenever I simply placed events or dialogue where they naturally belonged a plausible picture emerged.

Particular Translation Choices

My aim in the style of translation was to render each section quite literally, and yet in a way that is highly understandable to the contemporary reader of English. The style I chose is on the less-formal end of the spectrum. The best illustration of this would be my choice in some instances to translate "who," when English grammarians would say "whom." In my opinion, "whom" has fallen out of use for most English speakers in the United States. The choice to lean heavily towards the informal reflects my desire to present the scriptures in language that is highly accessible to everyday people.

I should note that I followed the lead of Dr. David H. Stern, translator of the Complete Jewish Bible, in rendering the name "Judeans" where other translations read "Jews." For a multitude of reasons I judged the term "Judean" to be a more accurate equivalent in current English usage than the word "Jew," which carries a multitude of meanings incompatible with first century realities.

I rendered some place names without explanation or alteration, like "Praetorium." I chose to use the Arabic word for "seasonal spring" in John 18:1 resulting in the name, "Wadi Kidron." It seems to me that "wadi" has come into English usage to such an extent that most readers would know what that meant.

    My blended translation of these passages is in no way meant to replace the reading of the actual standard translations of the Bible. I simply put the accounts together in this form as a way of helping you live through the last day on earth of the life of Jesus in your mind and in your heart. If my narrative strikes you as odd, or out of place, or inaccurate to what you believe happened, then I urge you to get out your own Bible and read the sections in question.

In Gratitude

In looking back over this project I see the imprint of many people who helped along the way towards the development of this book. I am grateful for those who encouraged me but also pushed me, challenged me but also made concrete suggestions, or disagreed with me but continued to listen.

I am grateful to numerous Sunday school teachers who loved me enough to not let me remain with my surface ideas.

I am grateful to various language professors who shaped my understanding of the whole nature of translation.

I am grateful to my pastor from University days, Dr. Steve Hayner, for seeing beyond the surface of things and courageously pointing to hidden realities.

Many translations of the scriptures are listed in the *References* section. My translation was made in consultation with those translations without any instances of copying their work. In a very few instances The Complete Jewish Bible, by David H. Stern, contained some unique and insightful renderings of particular words in English. My translation reflects my agreement with him, that these are the most accurate English representations of the underlying Greek text.

I wish to thank Dr. James Edwards for his invaluable comments on an earlier draft of this manuscript. His insights helped to greatly improve the final form. Any remaining flaws are, of course, entirely my own.

I especially want to thank:

Annie Zimmerman

I am married to the most insightful reader of the Greek New Testament that I know. On countless occasions she has opened my eyes to the subtle nuances in the text. Sometimes it has been by showing me small grammatical points that make a huge difference. Sometimes it has been through pointing out thematic elements that tie the whole narrative together. By simply being awake to the exact meaning, she has taught me. And she has inspired me from time to time by pulling out the Greek vocabulary flash cards, still retained from seminary days, and refreshing her abilities. I have made an effort to keep up my Greek in part because she has demonstrated it is possible.

Sue Hinkle

When I was in the first grade my Sunday school teacher found a way to explain that Jesus died to forgive my sins. I understood what she was saying, to the extent that a 6 year old is able to understand such a thing. Sue Hinkle was devoted to making the story of the suffering and death of Jesus real to

In Gratitude

children. I knew, from how she communicated the grace of it, that this was good news, and a relief from any suffering I might ever face. Her commitment to telling this story has given me a lifelong passion for communicating the love of Jesus so that our minds and hearts will understand. Sue has passed away but she continues to represent for me all of those humble messengers who "love to tell the story of Jesus and his love."

The Churches That Have Nurtured Me

I am grateful to all of the churches that have walked with me along the way. Since the story of the last 24 hours of the life of Jesus is the second most important story that anyone who is part of a church must know, I feel my capacity to tell it again must be partly due to their faithfulness.

Among all of the churches I am especially grateful to–

–West Side Church in Richland, Washington, for telling me this story throughout my years of growing up.

–Tualatin Plains Presbyterian Church in Hillsboro, Oregon, for allowing me to develop the "Stations of the Cross" path as part of Good Friday observance.

–Gateway Presbyterian Church, in The Dalles, Oregon, and Cedar Creek Church, in Sherwood, Oregon, for allowing me to further develop the Good Friday story when I was part of your pastoral leadership teams.

–Chapel by the Lake in Juneau, Alaska, for hosting the premier performance of *Down The Last Road* as a Readers Theater performance. Special thanks to Emily Fergusson for her masterful work directing the premier.

References

Aharoni, Yohanan, and Michael Avi-Yonah. *The MacMillan Bible Atlas*. New York: MacMillan Publishing, 1977.

Aland, Kurt, Ed. *Synopsis Of The Four Gospels,* Seventh Edition. Stuttgart, Germany: German Bible Society, 1984.

Aland, Kurt, Matthew Black, Carlo M. Martin, Bruce M. Metzger, and Allen Wikgren, eds. *The Greek New Testament*, 3rd. Edition (corrected). Stuttgart, Germany: United Bible Societies, 1983.

Bagster, Samuel & Sons. *The Analytical Greek Lexicon*. New York: Harper & Brothers, 1959.

Calvin, John. *Commentary On A Harmony Of The Evangelists, Matthew, Mark, And Luke*. Tr. William Pringle. Grand Rapids, Michigan: Baker Book House, 1996.

———. *Commentary On The Gospel Of John*. Volume One. Tr. William Pringle. Grand Rapids, Michigan: Baker Book House, 1996.

Cheney, Johnston M., and Stanley Ellisen. *Jesus Christ The Greatest Life: A Unique Blending Of The Four Gospels.* Eugene, Oregon: Paradise, 1999.

Chrysostom, John. *Homilies Of St. John Chrysostom On The Gospel According To St. John.* Translated and Edited by Philip Schaff. The Nicene and Post-Nicene Fathers, First Series, v. XIV. Grand Rapids, Michigan: Eerdmans, 1956.

Cullmann, Oscar. "The Plurality of the Gospels as a Theological Problem in Antiquity." Chapter 2 in *The Early Church: Studies In Early Christian History & Theology.* Edited by A. J. B. Higgins. Abridged edition. Philadelphia: The Westminster Press, 1966.

Dana, H. E., and Julius R. Mantey. *A Manual Grammar of the Greek New Testament.* New York: MacMillan, 1927.

deSilva, David A. *An Introduction To The New Testament: Contexts, Methods & Ministry Formation.* Second Edition. Downers Grove, Illinois: IVP Academic, 2018.

Dix, Gregory. *The Shape Of The Liturgy.* Second Edition. London: Dacre Press, 1945.

Edersheim, Alfred. *The Life And Times Of Jesus The Messiah.* Grand Rapids, Michigan: Eerdmans, 1971.

References

Edwards, James R. *The Gospel According to Mark*. The Pillar New Testament Commentary. Grand Rapids, Michigan: William B. Eerdmans, 2002.

Elowsky, Joel C., ed. *The Ancient Christian Commentary on Scripture: New Testament, IV b, John 11-21*. Thomas C. Oden, General Editor. Downers Grove, Illinois: InterVarsity, 2007.

Good News Bible: The Bible in Today's English Version. New York: American Bible Society, 1976.

Han, Nathan E. *A Parsing Guide To The Greek New Testament*. Scottdale, Pennsylvania: Herald Press, 1971.

Hoskyns, Edwyn Clement. *The Fourth Gospel*. 2nd ed., revised. Edited by Francis Noel Davey. London: Faber and Faber Limited, 1947.

Johnson, Luke Timothy. *Living Jesus: Learning the Heart of the Gospel*. New York: HarperSanFrancisco, a Division of Harper Collins Publishers. 1999.

Just Jr., Arthur A. *The Ancient Christian Commentary on Scripture: New Testament, III, Luke*. Thomas C. Oden, General Editor. Downers Grove, Illinois: InterVarsity, 2003.

KJV Giant-Print Classic Reference Bible. Grand Rapids, Michigan: Zondervan, 1994.

Kohlenberger III, John R., Edward W. Goodrick, and James A. Swanson. *The Exhaustive Concordance To The Greek New Testament.* Zondervan Greek Reference Series. Grand Rapids, Michigan: Zondervan, 1995.

The Lockman Foundation. *New American Standard Bible.* Carol Stream, Illinois: Creation House, 1973.

Major, H.D.A., T.W. Manson, and C.J. Wright. *The Mission And Message of Jesus: An Exposition Of The Gospels In The Light Of Modern Research.* New York: E. P. Dutton And Co., 1938.

Marshall, Alfred. *The Interlinear NRSV–NIV: Parallel New Testament In Greek And English.* Grand Rapids, Michigan: Zondervan Publishing House, 1993.

Marshall, I. Howard. *Commentary on Luke.* New International Greek Testament Commentary. Grand Rapids, Michigan: William B. Eerdmans Publishing Company, 1978.

———. *Last Supper And Lord's Supper.* Carlisle, U.K.: Paternoster, 1980.

Metzger, Bruce M. *A Textual Commentary On The Greek New Testament.* New York: United Bible Societies, 1971.

Morris, Leon. *The Gospel According To John.* The New International Commentary On The New Testament. Grand Rapids, Michigan: Wm. B. Eerdmans, 1971.

References

Nestle, Eberhard, and Nestle, Erwin. *Novum Testamentum Graece*. 17th edition. Stuttgart: Privileg. Württ. Bibelanstalt, 1953.

Oden, Thomas C.., and Christopher A. Hall, eds. *The Ancient Christian Commentary on Scripture: New Testament, II, Mark*. Thomas C. Oden, General Editor. Downers Grove, Illinois: InterVarsity, 1998.

Ogilvie, Lloyd John. *The Cup of Wonder: Communion Meditations*. Wheaton, Illinois: Tyndale House, 1976.

Plummer, Alfred. *An Exegetical Commentary On The Gospel According To St. Matthew*. Grand Rapids, Michigan: Eerdmans, 1953.

Rat der Evangelischen Kirche in Deutschland. *Die Bibel oder die ganze Heilige Schrifte des Alten und Neuen Testaments*. Vienna, Austria: Österreichische Bibelgesellschaft, 1976.

Robertson, A.T. *A Grammar Of The Greek New Testament In The Light Of Historical Research*. Nashville, Tennessee: Broadman, 1934.

Simonetti, Manlio, ed. *The Ancient Christian Commentary on Scripture: New Testament, Ib, Matthew 14-28*. Thomas C. Oden, General Editor. Downers Grove, Illinois: InterVarsity, 2002.

Stern, David H. *Complete Jewish Bible*. Clarksville, Maryland: Jewish New Testament Publications, 1998.

Strong, James. *Strong's Exhaustive Concordance Of The Bible*. Nashville, Tennessee: Thomas Nelson.

The Trinitarian Bible Society. *The New Testament: The Greek Text Underlying The English Authorised Version of 1611*. London: The Trinitarian Bible Society, 1976.

Holy Bible, New Living Translation. Wheaton, Illinois: Tyndale House, 1996.

The Holy Bible, New Revised Standard Version: Containing The Old And New Testaments With The Apocryphal/Deuterocanonical Books. New York: Oxford University Press, 1989.

Wilson, Neil S., and Linda K. Taylor. *Tyndale Handbook Of Bible Charts and Maps*. Carol Stream, Illinois: Tyndale House, 2001.

Zerwick, Max S.J. *A Grammatical Analysis Of The Greek New Testament*. Translated by Mary Grosvenor. Unabridged 3rd. Rev. Ed. Rome: Editrice Pontificio Istituto Biblico, 1988.

The *Down The Last Road* series

What started as a single blended translation has grown into four publications designed to make the story easy to use for individuals, for families, and for churches. This series of resources has been developed in order to present this story in the best possible ways for different audiences. Consider how you might use these to present this narrative in ways that will serve various needs. Whether sitting quietly alone, simply reading the simple story, or encountering narrative in other creative ways, you can make this day in the life of Jesus a life-changing part of how you see the world. Four different publications are available to make the meaning of this story more vivid in your experience.

Down The Last Road
The Last Day of the Earthly Life of Jesus

This blended narrative presents a complete account of everything the Gospels report concerning the last day of the earthly life of Jesus. Included in this volume you will find a simple, meditational version of the narrative, along with *Study Notes* with all of the scripture references included in detail.

This book presents the basic form of the narrative that is used for each of these resources.

Scenes From The Last Journey
14 Points On The Way of the Cross

The 14 events recounted in this book come directly from the pages of the four gospels. So these are not identical with the traditional 14 stations, but rather our 14 stations have been designed to reflect the Biblical accounts from the betrayal and arrest until Jesus is laid in the tomb.

Coming In 2022

THE LAST DAY

A PLAY IN TWO ACTS

This script contains the complete narrative of that last day, from just before the last supper up to the moment when the remaining friends of Jesus walked away from his tomb. The script was created straight from the text of the blended translation contained in *Down The Last Road*. All quotations were simply converted into spoken parts for the characters in the play. A narrator's part utilizes the precise words from the Gospels to set the scene for the dialogue that takes place.

The play is designed to be presented as a Readers Theater performance, so no costumes, sets, or line memorization is required.

Separated into two Acts, the play may either be presented all at once, or in two separate performances. Act 1 covers the events of Maundy Thursday, from the Upper Room to the arrest in the garden. Act 2 moves to the trial, abuse, and crucifixion. With a little planning you will be able to perform either a two Act play on Maundy Thursday, or put on two separate performances on Maundy Thursday and Good Friday.

For the sake of facilitating performance, the script will be available in two forms.

The Last Day

Director's Script

With extensive instructions, suggestions and notes, the Director's version of the script covers everything a director will want to know to lead a group of readers to perform the play. This will guide your preparations and help you know how many copies of the Reader's Script will be needed.

The Last Day

Reader's Script

This contains the simple script in two acts. To perform the reading, order enough copies to give one to each participant. The number of participants may vary based on how you choose to divide the readings. Guidance for this is found in the Director's Script, and it will be helpful to read that guidance before determining the number of Reader's Scripts to order for your performance.

Look for these scripts to be available in time for Holy Week of 2022.

ABOUT THE AUTHOR

Richard P. Zimmerman is a pastor and writer who has served in several congregations in the Pacific Northwest and Alaska. He holds degrees from the University of Washington (B.A.), Princeton Theological Seminary (M. Div.), Regent College in Vancouver, B.C. (Th. M.), and Columbia Theological Seminary (D. Min.). He also completed a year of advanced study in Northwest Semitic Languages at the University of Chicago.

Having a special interest in the languages of the Bible world has led him to take extensive courses in Greek, Hebrew, and related languages.

Richard makes his home the Pacific Northwest with his wife, Annie. They enjoy hiking, skiing and snowboarding, golf, and just generally being outside in God's creation.

ALSO BY RICHARD P. ZIMMERMAN

Walk With Me To Another Land: A Narrative Approach to Transitional Ministry

Launch: A Guide For The Season of Lent

www.ingramcontent.com/pod-product-compliance
Lightning Source LLC
Chambersburg PA
CBHW051401290426
44108CB00015B/2107